Broken

LOVE CHRONCLES
VOLUME 1 / THE ART OF LOVE

Araina D. Thompson

authorHOUSE®

AuthorHouse™
1663 Liberty Drive
Bloomington, IN 47403
www.authorhouse.com
Phone: 1 (800) 839-8640

Published by AuthorHouse   07/19/2016

ISBN: 978-1-5049-6199-8 (sc)
ISBN: 978-1-5049-6198-1 (e)

Print information available on the last page.

DEDICATION TO MY CHILDREN

Thank you for being forgiving as we grew up together.
Thank you for the love you showed and the growing
pains you gave. I will always be dedicated to all of you.
To my sister for listening to me read to her
over the phone every day for the past five
years, for her ideas and thoughtfulness.
Thanks must be given to GOD, for without
him there would be nothing.

HONOR GOD, THY SELF BEFORE OTHERS!

"To every little girl; who will one day grow into a woman?"

Please be smart about the love you choose. First and foremost, outside of GOD, your parents, and family, love is not unconditional. Be patient and gain understanding of what love is. Know that you cannot love or be loved by anyone else until you have first loved yourself

"To every little boy; who will one day grow into man?"

Please be smart about the choices you make and the babies you help to create. You want to first be a man. To understand what a man is, look in the mirror and ask yourself: are you the kind of man you'd want your daughter to bring home for a husband? You are a leader and to understand leadership you must understand GOD.

Jimmy and Brooklyn are high school sweet hearts. They have a loving relationship that turns them into parents. Jimmy is a football star on his way to college. He leaves a pregnant girlfriend. Jimmy and Brooklyn stay together through college.

They are married and they live a good life. Jimmy lives outside of his marriage and has several children. Can love hold them together? Can love supersede all the lies and deceit? Jimmy's friend Kevin listens and watches his best-friend loose his family and decides he is best suited for the part of Brooklyn's husband. He waits and watches until he feels the moment is right. Can he convince Brooklyn he is a better man for her? Brooklyn has run into an old friend who makes her feel appreciated and loved. He cares for her and wants to be with her. He is a billionaire and capable of giving her everything.

Will she leave Jimmy for someone that will love and respect her? When all three men meet face to face, they only have one thought on their mind: Brooklyn is *mine*.

Jimmy, Kevin, Jeff and Brooklyn square off in the streets while Jimmy and Brooklyn's daughter watches.

CONTENTS

FOR THE LOVE OF GOD

In the name of the father the son and the holy spirit I thank you for my life, health and strength and that of my children and all generations that come after me to be bless by your grace to fore-fill what is set before them, the true meaning of love: Amen.

Chapter 1

MOMMMY AND DADDY

Golden brown like a pecan kissed by the sun is the color of her skin and her eyes are as green as leaves on trees in the springtime. Her hair flows like waves in the sea. Her body is overflowing with curves and all the men love her. My mother is a very beautiful woman: her eyes stop every man she looks at. When she walks away, her ass gives them something to remember. 38-24-42 was the number she played and the shape she'd carried from age 12. On the weekends it was her, and me, daddy, and my brothers and sisters. Some his, some hers, only three of us are theirs together. I am the oldest of 7 kids between the two of them.

My daddy is a tall man that's 6'7ft, brown skin with brown eyes and big muscles. He lifted weights daily to show mama that what she had, every woman wanted. He is right. Every woman, whether she had a man or not, wanted my dad, and sometimes, a lot of times, he didn't say no. Seeing all the kids he had that weren't my mothers'!

My daddy could never deny any of his sons outside of his marriage because they all look just like him, every one of them and every time a child was born my ma could tell if it was his.

According to her she'd say, "Jimmy when ya looked down at that baby, was it like looking in the mirror?"

He'd say, "Yes Brook. I was looking in the mirror.

Mama was 5'7 and 145lbs of muscle with no fat anywhere. She worked out too but in different way. Sometimes they fought.

"One of these days Jimmy, I'm gonna give up this good sweet tast'n pussy to someone else and you will know how it feels. You always hurting me, always out there with them nasty ass women. You dirty fuck."

"The world will have lost the best pussy it ever produced." Jimmy said. "Ya hear me Brook? I'll kill you and the bastard ya fucking. You understand?"

Their fights started when I was about 6 years old. Sometimes I could hear them making love for a long time. Our house wasn't small; they were just loud. I wondered what he was doing to her to make her scream and holler likes that. He sounded like a roaring tiger. It scared me. One night my mama started screaming.

"You are a bastard! You fucking bastard, why you must go and do this to me? You make me sick Jimmy! You make me sick! Get the fuck out! Damn it!" She screamed. "Get the fuck out. I hate you. Don't come back no more."

"Woman I ain't going nowhere." I heard daddy say. "I am staying here with you and Althea, ya my family. You don't understand what it is to be a man. Those women be coming on to me and sometimes I get tired of saying 'no, I gotta woman.'"

"Fool I ain't just your woman! I am your wife."

I heard a glass smash and a thump. I hid under the bed. Then I crawled to the door of my room and peeked out. I saw my daddy coming out of the room holding his bloody head and mama on the floor, where he left her, out cold. I waited by my door until daddy went into the basement of our house. When he went down there, sometimes he didn't come up for a few hours, or for as long as he thought mama was mad, sometimes that could be days. He never left her, no matter how much she'd beg, he never left her. All the women I seen daddy with, none of them looked as good as my mama and he knew it. She was the best looking woman in our town and towns miles off. Daddy wasn't about to let another man have her.

"Mama, Mama is you all right? Mama- Mama?" I'd call her name and shake her. I'd go down stairs, make sure daddy wasn't in the kitchen, get some cold water out of the fridge, and throw it on her.

"You fucking bastard I'm a kill you!" She'd wake up screaming throwing her arms and kicking her legs.

"Mama it's me Althea. Daddy is gone now! It's just you and me."

"Oh baby I am so sorry." She put her hand to my face. "Althea you okay?"

"Yes mama I am." I said this time. "Why are you and daddy fighting? Don't you love him? Why you want him to get out?"

"I do love your daddy; he loves me and other women too. You got a brother and he ain't my son."

That's when Jaden was born. Daddy stayed in the basement for a week. The basement was a nice place though; he wasn't missing anything. He had a phone down there different from our upstairs phone. There was a kitchen and a bathroom, a living room, a pool table, and his computer. He could go in and out without coming upstairs. He had his own entrance.

The basement was where they played cards with his friends and sometimes mama and her friends would be down there drinking and smoking all kinds of cigarettes. The ones she didn't smoke in front of me made mama laugh and cry, especially when daddy would come home with news of his sons.

By the time I was 10 my daddy had two sons by two different women and mama was pregnant.

"Brook I looked in the mirror again and saw my reflection." He told her.

This time he said it while she was in the shower. She didn't respond to him. When she came out of the shower, she looked at him for what seemed to be a long time. I stood at the steps too scared to move. I didn't want them to tell me to go in my room. I wanted to hear what was going on, but I didn't want to get hit with whatever mama was going to throw at him.

She grabbed his hand and placed on her stomach. She stood there naked in front of him.

"Will it be born the same time our child is born? So you were out fucking someone else the same night you fucked me? Did you wash your dirty dick before you fucked me or is it possible that I wasn't enough for you and you went out for more pussy?"

Daddy dropped his head. Mama went in their room and daddy seemed too scared to follow.

"What you doing at the steps Althea? You listening to me and your ma have a conversation?"

"No daddy I was listening to you tell Ma, you got another baby." I said. "Why you so mean to her daddy? Why you got to have more kids and not with us? Daddy you always make mama sad." I told him. "I don't want to marry a man that will make me sad and make me cry all the time. You never make mama happy.

Now she is going to have a baby. What you gonna do with all these kids?"

Daddy just looked at me.

"Althea, will you stop asking questions baby girl? I'm sorry and yes you got another brother." "I hope it doesn't change things for me. Do I have to share a room? What's his name daddy? Does he look like Jaden?"

"His name is Jorden baby girl and he looks like Jaden. And they both look like you." He said.

"No they don't daddy. I look like ma daddy and you know it."

"You right baby girl. You look so much like ya ma it scares me. You're so beautiful and you filling out too." He smiled. "I don't know if I like that little girl."

"Why? Daddy" Cause I got breasts and a butt like Ma's?"

"Well, you almost got those things Althea. Don't be in a rush to grow up now."

"What daddy? You scared that men will want me, like you want those women even though you're married to ma?"

He looked at me as if I stabbed him in the heart.

"Althea please never ever let a man use you. Never let a man play you or dog you."

"Like you doing ma?" I said. "All the kids in school talk about how they mama sleeping with my daddy and this one say it and that one say it. You dogging my mother and I don't like it daddy. I love you but she should leave you or get a man that will love her back."

"Althea I do love your mother. I love her with all my heart. Don't I take care of y'all?"

"Yeah daddy, but you just said not to let a man dog me or hurt me, like you do ma. So what's the difference?"

"The difference is you my daughter and I am ya crazy daddy."

"Yep daddy you crazy' and Mama is even crazier for staying with you." I said.

"Althea you would leave me?"

"Yes daddy I would, I would not want to be with a man that brings home more children than he did groceries. Daddy you are a dog, but I love you."

"Little girl please don't grow up to fast, you going to make ya daddy kill somebody."

"Daddy you act like I'm still 6! I will be 11 soon and you got 2 kids and 2 on the way. I know how babies are made daddy. I know where they come from." I was standing in front of him feeling very grown up and sure of myself. He just put his head down like he always did. He walked down to the basement where I knew he'd stay for a week.

Weeks went by and then my daddy was back upstairs in their bedroom making love, and he stayed home more. He rubbed ma's belly all the time. We seemed like a real family. Jaden even started coming over on the weekends. He was 4 and tall for his age. He looked just like my daddy and thank god for that cause his mother looked like the grudge with nappy hair. She had a big ass, big tits, and a fucked up walk. She walked like she was drunk all the time. I suppose she missed my daddy, and then I wondered if daddy still made love with her. I thought to ask him one day.

The older I got, the stricter my father became. And the more he wanted to know where I was going, who I was with, who I was talking to on the phone or at the mall- my father was up my ass and he had started to get on my nerves.

Mama had twins: a boy and a girl. The boy died and mama damn near went with him, daddy cried all night and all day. And the next day the other woman had her twins. They both lived. She had a boy and a girl. Daddy dared not tell ma. It wasn't the right time (even I knew that). And ma had so many complications that, after the baby died, she stayed in the hospital for another 14 days, which meant daddy had to take care of me. 14 days seemed like two months. Daddy was a pain in my ass.

"Althea don't walk around like that, you need to be fully dressed when you come down stairs."

"Daddy, it's 7 in the morning. It's Saturday. Why I got to get dressed now?"

"Because, Althea, I told you to." He stood up.

"But- daddy, I want to sit and relax. I don't want to get dressed." I plopped down on the couch where he had been.

"But, nothing" Get dressed now." he yelled.

I laughed and went back upstairs to change.

"Is this better?" I had put on shorts and tank top.

"No. Put on some clothes girl"

Then it hit me. Daddy had noticed something I didn't -until I walked past the mirror and caught a glance of myself. I looked like my ma for real. My breast weren't as big as hers but they were growing and fast too! My butt was nice and plump not as wide as hers but it was up on my back and noticeable. My eyes were like hers. My hair was like hers and my skin color was just like my mother's. And for the first time, I realized how pretty I was. I was 11 years old.

I also realized that my father was never around on Saturday mornings. He was out with Jaden, Jorden, and probably one of their mothers. He usually returned around 9 or 10 and my mother made sure I was dressed by the time he got here. I had gotten my period when I was 10 and mama never told daddy it had came on and I had no pads. I had to tell my dad and I knew he wouldn't take it well. I really didn't know how to tell him, so I pretended I thought mama had told him already.

"Daddy, can you go to the store for me?"

"I need to go to the store for what althea?"

"Uh... for some pads" I said.

"Oh that's nice of you to think about your mother." He said. "But I'm sure she could pick those up on her way home."

"They're not for mom." I said.

"Who are they for?"

I didn't answer him and he asked again as he came up the steps.

He looked me in my face. "Who needs them Althea?"

"I do daddy." I said.

My father looked like he saw a ghost. He sat down at the top of the steps.

"How long have you been using pads baby girl?"

"A year daddy, didn't ma tell you?"

"No, she did not." He said and just sat there while I had tissue stuck up my ass.

"Daddy is you going?"

"Yeah baby girl, I'll go." He said.

He seemed sad and I wondered why. He came back from the store quick.

"Here you are Althea." He handed me the pads.

"Thanks dad." I said.

I thought for a moment. Finally I said, "Daddy I don't have any clothes you like."

"Want to go shopping then?"

"Yeah daddy I do."

In the mall I saw some of my male friends from school in the food court.

"Hey' Althea." Want to sit with us?" One of them asked.

"No she doesn't." my father said.

"Daddy, those are my friends!"

"No... They are *boys* and boys only want one thing."

"Daddy every boy isn't like you."

"Yes... they are."

"Well every girl ain't like ma."

"You right about that baby!"

"Daddy how old where you when you first had sex?" I asked.

"Althea, Nicole!" What in god's earth are you asking me that for?"

"I want to know. Ma said you and her had it at 16." I said. "I'm almost 16 you know...That's when I'll be having sex too."

My father picked me up and sat down.

"Baby girl," he said with tears in his eyes, "you don't need to have sex so soon."

"What is sex daddy? Is that when you make mama holler and you sound like a tiger?"

"Althea" He damn near screamed. "Let's go, you got everything you need and want?"

"Well, I do want another short set and more sneakers." I said

"Let's get them and go."

"Daddy you never answered me." I said "What is sex?"

"Ask your mother." He said

I tried on the clothes and came out and stood in front of my father. My father just stared at me and shook his head.

"Do I look cute daddy?"

"Yep" You look nice Althea." He said. "I see you're growing up little girl."

"Don't worry daddy. I'll always be your favorite girl."

"You are so innocent baby and I hope you stay that way for a long time." he said.

I had no idea what he meant by that.

Mama finally came home with my sister, Brooklyn, named after my mother. She looked like my dad and my mama, but more like daddy. She had his thick coarse hair, curlier than mine, big brown eyes and dimples like my daddy, and he loved her.

She is my little sister, someone I had to impress, to show her how to be lady, and show her what sex was. I had to show her how not to be played like daddy played mama. But first I had to find out what playing was, what sex was, and how not to get played. How was I going to find out?

By the time I was twelve mama had her son. His name was Jimmy after my daddy.

On a Saturday morning, my sisters and brothers and me: Jaden, Jorden, Brooklyn and the twins; Allen and Ayah. Jaden was 6, Jorden 5, Brooklyn and the twins were 2, and baby Jimmy was 3 months looking like his mama and me. He was pretty. I didn't get all the attention I was used to anymore. Things had changed a great deal. I now had to share a room with Brooklyn. It wasn't bad as I had first thought. She kept me company.

Jimmy stayed in the room with mama and Daddy. He would have his own room one day but he'd have to share it with his brothers when they came over on the weekends.

My father was overwhelmed with Ma's jealously. She started questioning his every move.

"Jimmy where you going? How long are you going to be gone? I'll have dinner ready by 6 will you be back in time to eat with us." She asked.

"No Brooklyn, I am going to Jaden's football practice with him."

"You *and* his mother I'm sure. Why haven't you asked us to go?"

"Brooklyn you know damn well that isn't a good idea. You know, as well I know, that would start some shit."

"No! You know as well as I know Jimmy this is the shit you started. Tell me are you still fucking that bitch?"

"What do you think Brooklyn? What the fuck do you think? Every time I go to one of the kids' outings I got to be fucking their mother. Look I don't have time for this bullshit. Why must you make it so fucking serious?"

"Why are you continuing to bring babies home? You got 7 kids. I only have 3. You tell me what is wrong with this picture.

You been dogging me for years and I am tired of it. You know damn well I don't trust you."

"You don't trust me? Look Brooklyn I am sorry. I know I fucked up and I am trying to make it up to you. All this bitching you doing is pushing me away. It's too late for all that. The kids are here. I am not going to neglect my kids because you got some emotional shit hanging on your shoulders. Leave me the fuck alone."

He slammed the door on his way out. My father never called my mother by her full name. He was definitely mad as hell. My poor sister kept answering him each time he said my mother's full name. That was funny. What wasn't funny was my mother's response to all his anger.

"Fuck his simple ass." She said. "I'm about to show him how it feels to be stepped on. You know Althea, most men don't know they been dogged until it's done. That motherfucker thinks his shits don't stink. Well baby, I'm about to show your daddy what it feels like to get played."

There was that phrase again: *getting played*. Damn what the hell does it mean?

"Ma what does getting played mean?" I asked.

"Well Althea your daddy has been playing your mama for years and sleeping with other women. Not caring about my feelings. Not caring how it makes me look. I am his wife. He doesn't respect it at all. What's the point of getting married if you continue mating outside of your marriage?"

She rambled on for what seem like an hour. The only thing I heard was: h*e is sleeping with other women*. I didn't hear the rest, maybe bits and pieces.

"Do you love daddy ma?" I asked

"Yes, baby I do. I have loved your daddy since I was 15 years old."

"How did ya meet ma?"

"Oh we met in such a beautiful way. We meet long before you were born; he was the safety on the school us. He is a few years older than me. I was in the third grade I think. Anyways those girls always wanted to fight me and your daddy always protected me. He wouldn't let any of them hit me. I loved him for that. As we got older he'd walk me to school and home every day. We became the best of friends. Your dad was popular in school. He was on the football team and the basketball team. He was an A student. Everyone loved your daddy, even the teachers."

"Tell me Ma. Tell me all about you and daddy-please ma?"

"Slow down Althea, after dinner we'll talk"

We soon said our grace and ate our dinner. Daddy hadn't gotten back yet. It was after 8.

Ma was pissed, but she didn't forget her promise. We cleaned up the kitchen together. Ma put dad's food in the stove for him. We bathed and crawled into her bed. Ma's tone lightens up. She seemed at ease now. She seemed relaxed. I started to understand how her mood changed. Tonight she didn't go in the basement to smoke her funny cigarettes. She was puffing away right in her room while my sister and I bathed. When we got in her bed you could smell the stench of the cigarette. She had candles lit and soft music played.

Chapter 2

WHEN THE LOVE WAS PURE AND INNOCENT

was younger than 10 when I realized who ya daddy was. He was always around;

I just never paid him any mind. These girls wanted to fight me every day.

"Brooklyn you think you are better than us." They said "you think because you got good hair, you prettier than us. We are going to beat yah ass bitch, to see if you can fight better than us."

"I don't want to fight yah. I just want to go to school. Yah leave me alone."

The kids in the back of the bus were laughing and edging the fight on. Then your daddy got on the bus.

"Don't worry about those girls. Brooklyn, I won't let them hurt you." He said. "You will leave Brooklyn alone. I don't want no fighting on this bus. You all will get sent to the office."

Everyone on the bus knew he meant what he said. All the boys were afraid of him because he was so tall, and much bigger than the other kids. All the girls loved him because he was so handsome. That went on for at least two years and the older I got the more the girls wanted to fight me.

When I was a little, Jimmy had an idea. We were walking from school.

"Brooklyn," He said. "Do you know why all the girls are jealous of you?"

"Why? Cause I'm with you? You are handsome Jimmy and Sexy." I smiled.

"Brook-do you mind if I call you Brook?"

"No Jimmy I don't mind."

"Well Brook all those girls are jealous because you look better than they do. Look at you baby; you are beautiful. You are sexy as hell. I can't believe I watched you grow up."

"I watched you grow up too."

"Yeah I guess so. Shit I ain't got any tits and ass. You don't realize how beautiful you are."

We were at my house. My parents weren't home as usual. Your Aunt Tamara and Aunt Misty were out back playing. Mama didn't mind him coming in. he never went up stairs until that day, and I took your daddy up stairs to see my room.

"Wow! Your room is fat Brooklyn, I mean Brook. Purple is your color. I like green on you though. Yep, green would match your eyes."

My room was purple white and sea green. I had purple and white walls. The left side was purple, the right green, the back wall purple, the front green and the trim and ceiling were white. My floor was hard wood with throw rugs, some green some purple.

That day I had on a sea green dress, with the back out and I had on white sandals.

"Look in the mirror Brook."

I walked over to the mirror. Jimmy came up behind me and touched my hair. He put his arms around my waist.

"Look at you. You are so pretty."

He untied my dress at the neck and let it fall on the floor. I was half naked in front of a boy for the first time.

He whispered in my ear. "You are indeed gorgeous. Look at you damn you are so sexy."

He touched my breast and rubbed his hands down my stomach onto my thighs. He turned me around, pulled me into his arms, and kissed me. His penis was stiff in his pants and it seemed very big, long and thick. My mind was racing.

"Brook I have never been with a girl. Have you been with a boy?"

"No, I'm not allowed to have a boyfriend until I am finish high school."

"You make me so excited Brook. Every time I look at you I get excited. Every time I touch you I get excited. Seeing your body makes me want you so bad."

He kissed me on my neck and my juices started to flow. I wanted something. I just didn't know what.

I heard my sisters' voices coming closer to the house. I pulled my dress up and we return to the kitchen. I poured him some cool aide and we stared at each other for a long time. I walked him to the end of my block.

"Thanks for walking me home. I like the way you protect me Jimmy."

"Did you like the way I made you feel, when we were in ya room?"

"Yes Jimmy you made me feel different. I can't describe it because I never felt that way before. I felt like I was your girl."

"You want to be my girl Brook?"

"Yes, do you want to be my man Jimmy? I'm not allowed to have a boyfriend until I finish high school I told you that. That's not until June, the end of June."

"I will wait for you."

"Jimmy I am a virgin."

"Okay, so am I. You'll be my first and I'll be yours."

"U Promise me Jimmy?"

"I promise Brook."

He kissed me on the lips, soft and long. My legs started to bend and he held me up.

"I want you so bad Brook, I can't control myself around you."

"My neighbors are going to tell my parents."

"Will you get in trouble?"

"Depends on what they say."

"I'll pick you up in the morning okay."

The next morning my mother questioned me about Jimmy.

"Brook is Jimmy your boyfriend." She asked.

"No mother he is not; not yet."

"Not yet? What does that mean?"

"He'll be my boyfriend when I am done school."

"That's a little over a month Brooklyn."

"It's okay right? We talked about this."

"I just want you to be careful Brooklyn. I don't want you in any trouble young lady. You are doing well in school. I want you to finish and go to college, or at least get some sort of trade."

"I will mama."

"We need to talk about protected sex. Do you know what that is?"

"No, I don't."

The doorbell rang.

"That's Jimmy mama I gotta go."

"Have a good day."

"Good morning Brook. Did the neighbors tell your parents? "Jimmy asked once I was outside.

"I think so. My mama asked was you my boyfriend?"

"What did you tell her?"

"I told her you'd be my man after graduation. Jimmy you'll be my man really soon, I'll be 18 and you'll be 19 years old."

"I realize that. It doesn't mean anything. I'll still wait for you."

"You won't be with another girl?" I stopped to look at him.

"I haven't been with another girl yet. Brooklyn there isn't a girl in our neighborhood that looks like you. I'm not going to blow my chance with you for them."

"I love you Jimmy."

"I love you too Brooklyn."

We sat on the bus together. We always had, but that day he played in my hair. He kissed me on my neck. He rested his hands on my stomach.

"Jimmy what you doing?"

"I smell you. You smell so sweet. I love the way you smell."

"Everyone is watching us."

"So, let them watch. You are going to be my girl. They should know now. That way none of them get hurt."

You could hear the girls whispering, *she can't be fucking him.* Another one said, *yes she is. He wouldn't be all over her for nothing.*

Jimmy stood up then. "I am with her because she is a nice person and a good girl. She looks better than all the girls on this bus. She is going to be my girl and my wife. Now shut ya fucking mouths up and ride the bus.

From that day to this one everyone knew me and Jimmy was together.

It was his last year in high school. I didn't know how much things would change after he left for college.

On my birthday my parents threw me a party I'd never forget. Jimmy was a part of it. At the end of the party a group of us went out to dinner and to great adventures.

We stayed at a hotel in NJ. In that hotel Jimmy became my man. He asked me to be his woman in front of the whole group.

"Brooklyn!" he called my name. He was standing at the front desk where they check in, calling me out loud, across the lobby. I walked up to him.

"Brooklyn, would you be my girl? I promise to respect you, protect you and love you."

"Yes Jimmy I will."

When all the kids went to the amusement park, we stayed behind. He was the only one with his own room. He invited me in.

"Brooklyn, you're damn near old now, how does it feel?" He said and closed the door.

"I don't know. I feel like I did yesterday, except you asked me to be ya lady. That was the best part of the day." Can you believe it?; We grown now. "We both laughed out loud.

He pulled me close and kissed me. He unbuttoned my shirt. He was surprised to see that I didn't have on a bra. He sat on the bed and pulled me even closer.

"Damn you are so sexy girl. Can I have you? Can I touch you?"

"Yes Jimmy you can have all of me."

He touches my breast and with his fingers encircled them. He kissed and sucked them.

My whole thought process stopped, juices started to flow, and I felt warm inside. Hot all over.

He pulled my shorts down. He picked me up and laid me on the bed. He continued to suck my breast. He kissed down to my love spot. He sucked it and kissed it until I moaned. I couldn't help myself. "Oh my God, Jimmy! Oh my god" I screamed.

"I want you Brook. I won't hurt you, I promise."

"Okay-" I panted trying to contain my rapid breathing. He took his clothes off. His penis stood straight up to the ceiling.

"What the hell is that Jimmy."

He could tell I was scared.

"Oh baby it's me. It's my dick, big isn't it?"

"I don't think it will fit."

"It will fit, and I won't hurt you. At least I hope not."

He found my hole.

"Damn you're wet and tight." He said as he maneuvered around. He finally got some of it in. A sharp pain shot up my stomach, as he entered me.

"Ouch! That hurt!"

"You okay?"

"Yes, I'm okay."

With each stroke he went in deeper. He went slowly at first, until we had a rhythm going. I moved the way he moved. When he pushes in I pushed in. When he pulled back I pulled back.

Soon I could feel something taking over me. He felt so good, I screamed.

"Yes Jimmy, yes Jimmy."

And to my own surprise he moaned and moaned louder and louder and we starting bumping like rabbits. Then it was over. We laid sweating and panting like overheated dogs.

"You okay." He looked down at me. "You're bleeding Brook." I was. I sat up.

"I guess so; you are so big. I never saw a penis before. Got damn you are *huge*."

We laughed. And we played. We took a shower together. His penis rose again and I gave him what he needed to put it down.

It was kind of funny the way I was walking. I hoped my ass didn't stay sore. I needed to walk normal before we I got home. My daddy would hit the roof and Jimmy) if he even thought I had sex.

We made love before school and it was so good. We made love every day after school. We got better at it. It lasted longer and I loved him. By the time I finished school, I found myself pregnant. Jimmy picked me up an hour before school. I left school at 12 noon to go to my pretend job. Jimmy gave me money every time he got paid. My girl friend Treshia worked at Macy's and made sure that my parents believed that I had a job there too. Before school we'd go to his parent' house and make love.

After school we'd go to his parents' house and he'd cook for me, feed me and then sex me. One Friday after school jimmy picked me up. Lunch was done cooking. We ate and went to Jimmy's room.

"Brook, guess what. I got accepted to the college. I'll live on campus for two or four years."

"What about us Jimmy? I'm pregnant."

"You're pregnant, what? Oh my goodness, Brook we are going to have a baby?"

"Jimmy you about to leave me. What am I going to do without you? You're happy I'm pregnant? My parents are going to kill us. My mom has stressed over and over again the protection that we have yet to use."

"Brook, it's too late for all that now, not unless you don't want to keep the baby." I hadn't thought about that.

"It's our baby Jimmy; yes I want to keep it. I just don't want to go through it by myself."

"You won't, you'll come to college with me the -baby and you. What do you think? You can become a nurse like you always wanted and I'll be a successful businessman." He held my hand. "We gotta start somewhere." he said. "We can't just be anything because we are going to have a baby. We got to finish our education more so now than before."

"Well, I don't know how to tell my parents."

"I'll go with you. I'll marry you, and next month when your finish school you come live with me in the dorm. We'll find a daycare."

"You got it all figured out don't you Jimmy?"

"It's easy baby when it comes to you. Long as you with me it don't matter how hard it gets. Nothing would be harder than not having you with me. I'll come home every weekend. I'll come home when you got to go to the doctors. You know I love you. You know you are the only girl for me."

We went to the doctors and the baby was due on my birthday. We made future appointments. The doctor only wanted to see me once a month. He gave me vitamins to take daily and I would need to have a test done in my 5th month.

"Now that was easy Brook, the hard part is telling your parents. Your pops is going to hit the roof."

"Jimmy as long as you understand that he is going to be very upset."

We entered my house. My parents were not surprised when Jimmy walked in. They were in the kitchen.

"Are you two hungry, baby girl?" My father asked. "We made ya favorite: fried chicken, greens, rice, corn bread, and sweet potato pie."

"Yep we are hungry." Jimmy said. He sounded normal. "Mr. Thomas, I need to talk to you privately. Is that possible sir?"

"Sure it is Jim; you want to talk now or after dinner?"

"Um…after dinner." He thought about my dad putting his ass out before he could eat.

I laughed to myself. The food was good. My mom's could cook very well. My dad wasn't a bad cook either. We ate and my dad called Jimmy out to the back patio.

"Come on Jim lets have that talk you wanted."

"Yes sir."

"Mr. Thomas, I respect you as a man. I hope you don't look at me different after I say what I must say. Sir Brooklyn and I are pregnant. We want to keep the baby, and I just got accepted to a university. I am going for my masters in business and engineering. I would like for Brooklyn to continue school and come to college with me when she graduate so she could complete her nursing degree. I called the school and they have a daycare on site. Our baby could go there. I love your daughter Mr. Thomas; I am going to make her my wife. She makes me happy. I bought the ring before she told me we were pregnant. I hope you don't hate me sir."

"Jimmy slow down, son. I already know she's pregnant."

"She told you?"

"No son. Her mother did. You can look at her and see something ain't right. She is thicker, eating more and sleeping more. Look Jim I don't like it- at all. But what's done is done.

You just need to know that it isn't our baby. We are not the parents. I am not the daddy.

You are and you are the one who will take care of my daughter. You understand me son?"

"Yes sir. I understand"

"Okay then, you won't have any problems so long as you don't forget what I said. Come in here son and eat some more pie. You told your mother son?"

"Yes Sir, I told her, she was very upset, and then she cried and was happy."

"I guess that's what a woman does, they all cry. I have to hear Tara's mouth all night."

Inside, my mama wasn't stupid by a long shot.

"What Jimmy got to tell your dad, that he couldn't say in front of us?"

"I'm pregnant Ma."

"I know Brooklyn; I found your prenatal vitamins in your dresser. You eat like a pig and you sleep all the time."

"Ma is you going through my things

"Yep, be a fool not to. What happen to the protection we talked about?"

"I don't know ma, I guess I never thought about it after we talked."

"Dumb ass, now you stuck with a baby and you better hope that man loves you for life."

"Ma, he does and he will."

"Girl you are stupidly in love and nothing's wrong with that but getting knocked up at before marriage is real stupid."

"He has never been with another girl, and now he going to college and leaving you for a whole year. You think he's not going to get nothing from other women?"

"He won't cheat on me mama?"

"Okay you wait and see."

"Mama is there a reason why can't you just be happy for us?"

"Oh baby, I *am.* But it is not about me being happy. It's about you being smartly happy. Don't expect that man to be with just you. He's young. He hasn't seen real women yet. When he gets to college those girls are going to be all over him and he ain't going to be able to say no all the time. I know- been there done that."

"How you know he's going to college?

"Brooklyn I am always listening baby, there ain't much I don't know."

High School was different after Jimmy left. The girls started picking on me again.

"It was good thing Jimmy was a boxer Althea. He taught me how to fight. He also paid for me to go to boxing school."

With that my daddy walked in the door and Ma rushed me and little Brooklyn out of the room.

"Ya'll go to bed now, I'll tell you more next time." She said and kissed us both.

"You promise ma? I want to hear the rest."

"I promise Althea. I will tell you more later on."

My dad came up the steps calling my mother's name. You could smell the stink coming up the steps before him. He staggered back and forth like Jaden's mother. He was drunk.

"Brooklyn" Where are you at?"

"I'm here. Where you been Jimmy? Oh God you been drinking!"

"I am so sorry Brook to have hurt you. I went to the bar -seen a few friends. Started drinking and here I am. I am so sorry. I never meant to hurt you Brooklyn. You are my first love. You are the only one I love. You hear me woman, do you hear what I am saying?"

"Come to bed Jimmy. No take a shower." She laughed.

When, my mom went into the bathroom with my dad, I went into their room. I don't know why, but I did. I stood there remembering the story ma was telling about daddy and her.

She really loved him. They had been together for a long time. I guess that's why ma put up with all his baby making stunts. They were coming out of the bathroom; I knew my parents would beat my ass if they caught me snooping around in their room. My parents had their own bathroom; there was nowhere to run, so I hid under the bed. There was a mirror in front of their bed, a big mirror. I could see everything.

Chapter 3

ALTHEA FINDS OUT WHAT SEX IS

My dad was naked and he crawled onto the bed. My mama was naked too. My father sat up. "Brook I am so sorry. I know I hurt you and I never meant to. I wish I could take it all back baby. I can't. I don't want to lose you. It hurts that you don't trust me. You have every right not to trust me. How can I gain your trust again? Tell me baby that it's not too late."

"Jimmy I don't know." I could barely hear her. She spoke so softly to him.

"You hurt me bad Jimmy. Not once but four times and why are you sleeping with those women without protection? They could give you a disease and then what? You give the disease to me? Jimmy I don't know how to live without you. I don't know how to live with you."

My parents were both crying and I wanted to cry too. They started puffing on mama's funny cigarette. They turn on the music. They started dancing kissing. Daddy did have a big wee-wee.

"Don't leave me Brook my. My boys talking shit saying you would soon leave me. Or start cheating on me. I'm the only man that's had this pussy. Brook I don't know how I would respond if another man was banging my pussy and sucking on my tits." My dad was still crying.

"Jimmy I don't want to be with another man. I don't want to know another man. Baby you all the man I need. I don't want to share you either." My mother was crying too. Daddy sat on the bed. And pulled my mama to him; he started kissing on her neck, and breast and my mama made these weird moans. He put his face down between her legs. She put her foot on the bed post. He kept sucking her and licking her. She threw her head back and called his name. Then she pushed him down on to the bed. She sat on his wee-wee and it disappeared. She went up and down and it looked like she was on a horse riding and daddy's eyes rolled into the back of head, Brook, Brook he yelled in between gasps of air. Then there came the tiger sound I usually heard, that woke me up some nights.

He flipped my mama over. She was on her knees and his big wee-wee disappeared in her butt, I thought. They bounced back and forth. Then I figured it out. The hole I have, Brooklyn has, all girls have and that has to be where he put it. How did it fit? Daddy was moving fast and mama was moving with him. They sounded like animals. Daddy smacked her butt.

"Nobody does it like you baby. Damn girl you making me harder Brook, I love you."

"Yeah daddy you love this pussy? Say it. You can't live without this pussy, say it mother fucker say it." She was calling him daddy.

He said it. *Whatever* she told him, he said it. Then he let out his tiger roar. And they fell onto the bed. When my daddy closed his eyes, I crawled out the room. I knew what sex was. Wow. I had all kinds of thoughts. Is that what my dad did to those other woman? He had to. They had babies. My door opened. My father came in and kissed me on my cheek.

"You missed dinner daddy."

"I know baby go to sleep. I see ya in the morn."

I wiped his kiss from my cheek. Seeing that daddy had just finish kissing mamas love spot, Eel! I didn't want him kissing me. I wanted to know if he kissed Jaden and Jorden's, or even the twin's mother's love spot like he did mamas. Ugh. I could hear them making love again. I could hear mama screaming.

"Suck it Jimmy; don't stop *please*."

She was begging him to suck her love spot. I heard my daddy's tiger roar. Every time I dosed off. I heard my mother call his name. I could hear my father's tiger roar and from that night on I knew what they were doing. I regretted invading their privacy but I wanted to know what made them make those sounds. The next morning at breakfast mama and Daddy seemed real happy laughing together. Daddy went off to work; mama is taking Brooklyn to daycare. I left for school.

It took mama a whole month to get back to her story about her and Daddy.

"School was fun for me. I didn't have a lot of friends. The friends I had would be for life. A few of them would be anyway. Without your daddy there every day, school seemed useless. The girls would pick on me. None of them knew I was pregnant and I am sure it would not have mattered much if they did. See, your daddy paid for me to go to boxing school. He made sure I could defend myself. I guess he knew it would be on and popping the moment he stepped out of that high school. Those girls were shocked the day I had to beat Lilly's ass.

It started on the bus.

"Where ya body guard at now Brooklyn? Who's going to protect you now?"

She pushed me.

"You know I don't like your ass. You laying up with Jimmy and shit. He should have been my man. What you going to do with a man like that? You ain't got any skills to keep a man like Jimmy."

Lilly kept talking all the way to school. I tried to ignore her. When we got to school she shoved me again in the hallway."

"Bitch- you just wait until school is over. I am going to beat that ass"

I tried to play her off. I knew I could beat her. I just didn't like to fight. I know why she was jealous though. Her man Craig was all up on me from the day Jimmy left. Right there in front of her in the hallway next to her class. I knew it was only a matter of time before she asked me to break her neck.

That day was the first and last time I had a fight.

Craig walked up to me.

"Brooklyn you know Lilly is going to try and fight you after school?"

"I am not worried about her at all."

"You're not? You're not scared of her?"

"No. Why? Should I be?"

"You're just so quiet all the time- Brooklyn I do like you. Hell girl you're pretty."

"Thanks Craig."

He leaned in to kiss me but I smiled and walked away.

When it was time to get off the bus, she pushed me off the bus.

I turned around and punched the bitch in the mouth for running it. I have her a two-piece, left than right. When the bitch started to fall, I landed a nice uppercut to her chin. She was out cold. I picked up my books and left. The group of kids that I left standing there had their mouths gaped open. They were in shock that I too could hold my own with or without your daddy. She never even got a chance to hit me. I laughed to myself as I walked home.

I never had a problem out of her or her big mouth friends ever again.

I missed your dad. He had been gone only a week. I called him a few times and he didn't return my call for days. When he did I was mad, remembering all the things my mother told me about men and Jimmy sleeping with other *real women*.

He tried to assure me that he wasn't messing around. I trusted him. I believed him.

Jimmy came back and forth as promised to see me to the doctors.

Soon Jimmy didn't want to go back up state.

"Brook you getting so big. Our baby will be here soon. I don't want to leave you."

He was rubbing my belly. Watching you move around. I was 5 months.

"Jimmy, babe you got to go back. Remember we can't stop now. I'll follow you in September. You know I won't start until January when the baby is older."

"Woman it will be cool just to come home to you. I miss you..."

"You were born July 28th. Your daddy was there, my daddy and mom, Jimmy's mom and dad and my two sisters."

"Girl they got on my nerves. Jimmy asked them to step out and give us some privacy."

The contractions had started the night Jimmy came home.

"Jimmy my water broke, I think."

"What you mean? Girl it is 3 am go back to sleep."

"Jimmy wake up."

The fool wouldn't wake up. The pains started in my back and rotated around my stomach. I thought maybe it would go away. After a while I couldn't take the pain anymore. I started to cry. I called my mom

"Mama my water broke, I think."

"When, what time did this happen?"

"It's been about a half an hour ago or more-ahhh."

"Honey where's Jimmy?"

"He Sleep. He won't wake up ma." I said through tears and groans.

"I will call the ambulance for you and meet you at the hospital."

The sirens got closer. The pain got closer.

Jimmy jumped up.

"What the hell is going on? Are you all right? Why are you crying? Oh my god is it time?"

"You wouldn't wake up. My stomach hurt so badly. It's the baby Jimmy it's coming out."

"What the hell you mean, right now?"

He ran to the door, back to the bathroom, to the bedroom, just running around in circles.

"What you want me to do? Do you want me to pick you up? Mom- Mom!" He started calling his mother.

"Your mom is at work Jimmy."

"Where's the phone? She'll know what to do."

"The ambulance is outside. Come on Jimmy it's time to go." Jimmy had to help me. I couldn't walk.

He picked me up. A contraction came. He put me down.

Thank god for the ambulance driver.

"I'll take over from here sir." He said.

They put me on the stretcher and put us into the ambulance. Jimmy hopped in too.

At the hospital, they wanted to examine me, it hurt so bad I screamed. What did I do that for? Well I don't know but your father freaked out.

"How the hell are you going up there when something is trying to come out? Do you know what you're doing? You should get another doctor." I put my hand over his. Finally he calmed down.

There was a whole lot of moaning and groaning and I was hitting your dad. Then there was pushing. I felt as if I had to have a bowel movement. Then here you came. Althea you were so pretty. You weighed 10lbs. Your dad just hugged and kissed you. He couldn't take his eyes off of you. The next day when you open your eyes and they were green line mine, he damn near died.

"Oh I see I'm going to kill someone over this little girl."

"Jimmy she ain't even 24 hours old yet."

We laughed. Both families were there and everyone was so proud of you.

We stayed with my parents until September. Jimmy was home every weekend. September came around fast. My mother was sad to see us go.

Living on a college campus with a baby was kind of hard. All the parties they had I couldn't go to the football games. Your daddy didn't want you there.

"Why, mama?"

"Althea he swore someone would try to steal you or the football might hit you."

He was crazy. By the time you were four. We were both finished school. We graduated basically at the same time. It took him 4 years and it took me two. Jimmy's internship hired him. It wasn't hard for me to get a job. We got our own apartment. One year later we bought this house. It was very hard for us for a long time. Your daddy did long hours at his job. I worked long hours at my job.

That was the last thing I heard her say, that night. I woke up in my bed.

My mom was not in her room. My dad wasn't in there either.

I went down stairs. The house seemed empty. I called the phone down stairs in the basement.

My dad answered.

"What's wrong baby? Why are you up? I'll be up there in a minute."

"Daddies where is mommy?"

"She asleep isn't she?"

"No, daddy she isn't in here".

My mother walked into my room.

"Althea what you doing out of bed young lady?"

"Mommy I couldn't find you."

"I was in the bathroom. You're worse than your father. Come and go to bed."

My dad went back down stairs with his friend Kevin.

"Jimmy, everything's ok?" Kevin asked.

Chapter 4

HOW JIMMY AND KEVIN MEET

Kevin was my man from college. He was the first person to greet me at my dorm. He was my roommate. Kevin is 6'4 and about 210 pounds. He is a dark skin brother and all the ladies love his chocolate ass. He was a player in college but he kept his grades on point and started his own trucking business after college. He owns a few laundry mats and lives alone. He doesn't have any children and never seemed to want a steady relationship with anyone. He always dated about 3 different girls at the same time. And they always know about each other. He claims none of them were right for him.

Kevin was on the basketball team and chose not to go pro. He played football the last few years of college and was good at it. He didn't want to go pro in that sport either. He's is pretty set financially, his house is paid off. Plush shit is everywhere. He's a loner and enjoys his single life. I personally think he's lonely. I know I catch him looking at my wife a lot. I don't really like it but I can't control his eyes and my wife *is* beautiful. I hope he knows that I'll kill his ass if he ever crosses the line. He knows I am a cannon and I will most differently blow up. He's cool though, I just have this weird feeling when Brooklyn is around.

"Jim is everything alright?"

"My daughter woke up. She's ok Brook got her."

"Yo man, let me ask you something? I've been trying to hold it in for years. Why you messing up? You're not happy here?"

"Yeah man I'm happy here. Why you ask?"

"Jimmy you got a good thing going on why you messing up man? Yo man, your wife is fine as hell. No disrespect intended. You be out there with them chicken heads and making babies. How long do you think you'll be getting away with this shit?"

"I am not getting away with anything. Brook knows what I have done and all the children I have."

"Jimmy you not understanding me? Let me ask you this? Was yours the first dick Brooklyn had?"

"Yes and the only dick too. I am the only man been in that. That is my pussy."

"Well Jimmy is it good?'

"Yo you're getting kind of personal."

"Naw Jimmy; I'm saying you act like it ain't working for you. You're everywhere else but here. You got more kids outside then in. She doesn't know how fine she is. She doesn't know that another man would come after her and respect her. She doesn't understand that there are other men outside of you. You got a dime piece on your arm you don't know it. And she doesn't know it."

"Look man, you sound like you want my wife."

"No. No. I am telling you something and you're not listening: your wife doesn't understand what she *is*. When she does you're gonna be hurt and bad too. You are doing shit you can't handle if done to you. That's all I'm saying man... that's all I'm saying."

"Kevin you right man. I would most def kill them all. If I thought my wife was cheating I'd snap her neck and the nigga I thought she was cheating with. It doesn't have to be true. I just gotta think it is. It's all over. Kev, man, I don't know what got into me. I don't know why I cheat. Once I started I couldn't stop. I guess my head got big. It's amazing how all the women wanted Jimmy. I ran with it and I couldn't get enough of it. Now I got all these kids and I love them. Brooklyn is so hurt and crying all the time. She even told me to get out a few times. She knows I am never leaving her and if so, only by death man. I love her. She knows I love her."

"Does she really know Jimmy? I'm down with you man. It's just that I would never step out on my wife. Well if I had one. That's why I'm not married. I want to do my thing. However when I do get hitched I am hitched for life man. She will be my one and only lover. So when the bitch cheats, I got good reason to blow her head off."

"You're crazy."

"Yeah well crazy you may call it. But you got the same mind frame. You're playing yourself. You can't get mad if she cheats. You started it. You started the whole thing. You even brought babies home and demand she accept them. You bring them in her face. Like so what I gave this dick up to someone else, deal with it and the shit droppings with it."

"Yo Kevin you are out of line man. I know you trying to check my brain and shit, but you're out of line."

"Look Jimmy I'm your boy. I will always tell you the truth. I'm the motherfucker that got your back right or wrong. You might not like the truth but it is what is and I am telling you one of these days that girl is gonna step out on you. You don't see it and I am here as your friend to show you what you don't see. Maybe it ain't too late, I am just warning you."

"Man she doesn't know about Karen or her being knocked up. I'm trying to get the woman to get an abortion."

"What jimmy you kidding me right? You already got 7 kids. Man one question just one?"

"Why the hell you keep knocking these bitches up ain't you ever heard of a fucking condom?"

"I know man I know. It just feels so good inside. You know the softest place on earth. I just can't seem to stay out of there."

"Jimmy this isn't no laughing matter."

"I ain't laughing. I am going to pay for an abortion and that's that. I am going to leave the woman alone. I got what you saying and I will try and leave well enough alone."

"Man you seem very laid back for a man that's about to lose his whole world. How long you have been doing this shit?"

"Man since we got into college. The moment I got there. These chicks were throwing pussy at me; the night I walked on campus. Man the shit was coming down like rain and my dick was the only pole outside. You act as if you don't remember. Man you was right there getting pussy in the same room I was. Man, don't act like you don't know."

"Jim, we were kids then. Even then you had a baby on the way. When she moved up there I thought you'd stop fucking them chicken heads. You were doing great. I saw you trying to be a family man. I saw you brush the chicken heads off and I took them all in."

"Kevin I gotta be honest with you and what I am about to say won't justify none of the shit I been doing. It's all wrong. Sit for a while man, I got a few beers and a nice blunt. I gotta check on my family. You roll the shit. I'll be back."

"How's the family doing by the way? Everybody cool upstairs?"

"Yeah everybody cool, I gotta do something give me a min. You need something?"

"Yeah Jimmy for you to hurry yo ass up, I gotta know the demon in you."

"Well, drink up, some and I'll be back. Yo Kevin, catch the remote; do you."

Upstairs Jimmy found his family all in one room with Brooklyn reading to her children.

He stood at the steps listening to them.

He thought to himself:

Brooklyn is a good mother, a good wife, a great lover. I don't why I cheat, she is so beautiful, and Kevin is right. I know this isn't right any man would want her... probably do right by her too. Shit would kill her if she knew about Karen, what if this woman doesn't get the abortion, and then what? Brooklyn will never forgive me. Althea is too old for the shit to be thrown in her face. Eventually she'll hate me too. She is already asking too many questions about boys and sex. She got her damn period and her ass is huge along with her tit's they are bigger than some of the bitches I look at. God please help me be a better man, father and husband. Then there's little Brooklyn and Ayah, what will they think of me. I sure couldn't handle any man treating my daughters this way. Oh shit, Kevin is waiting on me…

"Yo Kevin it smells good down here. Did you save me any?"

"Hell no man, you took forever and day. What the hell were you doing?"

"Yo its cool Kev, I got some more, look in the trunk you resting your feet on."

"Kevin, on a serious note, I was upstairs listening to my wife read to our children. Brooklyn is a very pretty woman and she enjoys being the mother of my children. I do love her Kev; I just have fucked up ways."

"Well Jimmy, roll and tell the story."

"I will never forget the day I recognized how pretty she was. She stepped up into the bus and her eyes caught mine. I took notice of how smooth her skin was and how pretty her eyes and smiles was. I knew she was mine. The little bitches on the bus kept picking at her. You know me, I had to let them know that was my girl and that's it, no more drama. I taught her how to protect herself and she taught me how to be patient for the pussy. We were smashing since we were young. It was my first time and her first time. Well it wasn't long after that, she got pregnant. It might have been a year. I had to go away to college most of her pregnancy but I came home every weekend and I made every doctor's appointment. Kevin, when I went to college and lived on campus it was all over. That is me being true and faithful to her. You remember the first 6 months every girl on the whole campus was like, who you? I was trying to stay focused on my studies and my girl and my daughter. Soon, girls were throwing it at me. I was finding myself in awkward situations. Man you know that shit was easy, pussy was everywhere, and I guess being the captain of the football team made it easy to get almost anything I wanted."

"I remember Jim you had a few problems with the fellas."

"Yeah man I remember because their girls where coming at you hard."

We both laughed

"Yo, Kevin this one chic in particular did not care that I had a family back at home. She straight told me."

"Her name was Tammy, nice body, smart too, no kids. You remember Tammy right?"

"Yo, Jim that's right the chick that was driving on her daddy's dime. She was pushing a brand new BMW".

"She told me her dad gave it to her. She kept her grades tight, so it was hers. She played it slick too, as if she just wanted to be friends. She'd come to our dorm to study. Math was her greatest threat. I agreed to help her and everyday she'd come over with a little more skin showing. One day she came over and was like you want to go swimming after we study. I said sure. Man this chic came out of her shorts and tank top right there, nothing on and wanting to use my bathroom too. I tried to fight it. She came at me hard."

"Jimmy, do you think I need to lose a little weight'?

'No, Tammy you look straight.' I told her.

"She stood in front of me naked. She grabbed my hand and put it right on her ass.

'Jimmy you don't think it's too much booty?'"

Kevin laughed and choked on the blunt.

"You're killing me, Jimmy. I remember she was bad as hell."

"Kevin, man you got to hear how this bitch handed me the pussy on a silver platter."

'Nah Tammy you got a nice body.' I told her. Before I knew it, I was rubbing her ass. She started moaning and shit, and then she took my hands and put them both, one on each tit."

"Man Kevin it was the fuck over. I tried to knock her brains loose. I fucked the shit out of that girl. She must have told some of her friends. Those girls were like I heard you got a nice package can we see. Pass the blunt man! -I'm talking about senior girls with experience- those girls taught me how to fuck and how to fuck well."

"I know what you're saying, them bitches put it on me like no other. Jim, I was a virgin when I got to college. I was on some shit like: 'I'm a save this dick for my wife.'"

I was on the floor laughing, choking, and trying puff at the same time.

"Oh, by the way, Kevin, you still ain't married yet, my dude. Man those girls taught me so much about sex that when I did get a hold of Brooklyn she didn't know what hit her. But she never accused me, not once. A year later I started backing up from the chic's because Brook was on her way there. I also knew the brothers would be all over her.

Well sure enough the day she steps on campus fools were all over her. I even had to take a step back. I couldn't believe how fine my girl was. She had filled out nicely after the baby. Remember we had to fight a few dudes? Once the nigga's knew she was mine, I went back to sneaking. It was like sneaking cookies from the cook jar, when your parents aren't looking, but if you get caught your ass is in trouble. It was the thrill of it all and I been sneaking that cookie ever since. None of them girls I slept with ever ratted me out. They weren't all that nice to Brooklyn either though. Kev, I never stopped loving her. I was just having fun."

"Jimmy, have you ever thought about getting caught? Did you ever stop to think you might be hurting her? When you did get caught, didn't you ever think that she might leave you? Why would you sleep with them girls without any protection? You could have brought back all kinds of shit."

"I know Kevin, well do I know. When Brook found about my son, she didn't say nothing. She cried for a while, but when she saw him, she instantly loved him. She even wanted to adopt him."

"What? She wanted to adopt him. She really loves you or she is crazy!"

"My dude, watch your mouth."

"Well Jimmy what you do you think she is going to do when she finds out about Karen and this new baby?"

"Kevin I really think she'll leave me. She has been crazy since we lost one of the twins. Man I think she'd walk out the door and that of course would break my heart. She is the only woman I've ever loved."

"You mean Jim, that shit would kill you."

"Yeah, it would. I cannot imagine another man fucking my girl."

"You mean fucking your wife."

"Yeah, I couldn't imagine another man fucking my wife. I must convince Karen this baby can't happen. I can't lose my family over some bullshit. It's going to be hard to convince this girl. She is happy has hell. She doesn't have any children and she's 35 years old. Man I don't know what to do. I know one thing, even if Karen had the baby, I couldn't bring it here. It would have to be a secret forever. He would never know the rest of my kids. Brooklyn would probably make me chose between this kid and her. I can't go through all this shit man this is crazy."

"Yo, Jim you think she would go that far."

"Hell, I don't know. She has been tripping lately. When I leave she questions me. When I go to my son's games she asks if I am fucking his mother too."

"Are you serious Jim, man you know shit is about to hit the fan. And it is your entire fault. You got the perfect set-up. Dudes like you make it hard for a brother like me."

"What you saying Kevin?"

"It's true, when we find a woman we'd even consider marrying, they got so much baggage from men like you, it is hard to stay with them. Then they are crazy acting with us. Assuming we are cheating, they bring the baggage you create with them and truly want us the good men to understand and here we are in divorce court...man, what are you going to do?"

"I am going to talk to Karen and see if she'd go through with this abortion and take it from there? Why, do you have any suggestions?"

"Yeah man; come clean with your wife. I am not saying tell her about this situation. I'm saying fix it. Then don't fuck up again. Brooklyn is going to leave you one of these times."

"I know I can't handle this shit man. Should she leave me, my whole world will crumble. I wouldn't know what to do without her. She is my life; she is what I live for. I can't believe I got myself into this shit again."

"Jimmy can I ask you a serious question? Was the pussy that good that you had to run up in it raw? Was it worth the risk of disease and yet a baby and the loss of your family?"

"Kevin, in the long run the answer is no, however, in the moment, Karen got some good pussy. Her body is off the chain and she will do anything and everything I tell her to do."

"Well what you saying, she satisfies you more than your wife?"

"No! You got me wrong. Brooklyn is, well, let's just put it this way, no other woman could compare. I'm just greedy and

I like the thrill of getting some, sneaking around turns me on. It isn't that she is better, or even looks better than my wife. It's the thrill of it all."

"Well," Kevin chuckled, "if Karen doesn't get the abortion. You will have the thrill of your life."

"I have to meet Karen tonight at 10. I am going to explain it all to her."

"Good luck man. Call me when you get in."

"I will walk out with you. Let me holla at my wife first.... 'Hey babe, I'm going to roll out with Kevin for a while okay!'"

"You mean you're going to roll over in some new pussy and Kevin is your excuse!" Brook yelled from her room.

"Yo man she is really tripping. Let's roll out of here."

While driving home Kevin thought:
Jimmy is a fool; I need a woman like that. I bet Brooklyn got some good pussy. I have wanted that ass since I met her in college. I actually love her. I just got to keep cool. I could kill Jimmy for treating her that way. Who the fuck does he think he is? He has everything and yet none of it is enough for him. He wants more and he is never satisfied. I got to play it cool because Jim is a cannon and I would have to kill him. Man if Brooklyn could love me back, I'd take him right out of here. Damn home at last. Jimmy is a selfish mother-fucker with all that talk about how good his wife is in bed. Finally at home, he stood at the door, pulled his pants down and began to stroke himself.

Oh yeah Brooklyn, Jim don't know how to give it to you like I do. Damn I wish I could have you.

Kevin moaned and pulled on his dick faster as he thought about Jimmy's wife. He was about to climax when there was a knock on the door, but he felt too good to move.

Yeah Brooklyn works that big ass umh-oohh oh yea...
The phone rang.

"Kevin, are you up man?"

"Jimmy this you, what up man is everything all right?"

"No man it isn't. I'm out in front of your house."

"Jimmy its 2 a.m. What the hell is going on? Oh shit, don't tell me. I'll be there in a min."

Kevin pulled up his pants, ran to the hall bath, and washed his hands.

"Come on in Jim; man what's the deal on Karen? Jimmy you crying? Aww shit, the bitch is keeping the baby? Tell me I am wrong. What the hell happened? Sit here man. Let me get you a beer- nah you need some Hennessey you want a shot?"

"Yeah man an eight-ounce shot. I can't believe this shit. I met Karen at her house. We talked for a while. I explained my situation."

"No, Jimmy tells me the way it really happened."

"All right man, look I sat Karen down, I said. 'Baby do you know for sure you are pregnant.'

"She said 'Yes.'"

"I said, 'Baby you know my situation. You know we can't have this baby. You know that I am married and it would not be a good thing to bring a child into this. I wouldn't be able to be a good father for this child. You'd be all alone in this. That's not fair to you or the child.'"

"She said to me. 'Look Jimmy boy, you should have thought about your wife and family and used a condom, since you didn't, you gave up your chance to make any other decisions. This is our baby and this child will be born. Now what you tell your wife is none of my concern. However, you will take care of this child. Look Jimmy I am not getting any younger. I want a baby. I can take care of this baby and I really don't need you. However I would like for my child to know his/her father and brothers and sisters.'"

"I tried telling her this, 'Karen this is not going to happen. My wife will have no part of this baby; she will not allow me to be in its' life. My wife will make me chose between this child and her.'"

"She said, 'well, Jimmy you got problems. I guess you must chose then. Like I said boo, when you chose not to wear a condom…Now if you don't mind I don't want to talk about this anymore.'"

"Man I just sat there looking at her. I got mad as hell; I grab the bitch by the throat and shook her. I threw her down on the floor. I threw a $1000.00 and told her 'either you get rid of it. Or here is the only money you will ever get out of me.' I slap the shit out of her and then left. I drove home and couldn't go in. I couldn't go and get in the bed with my wife knowing that tomorrow will be a nightmare. I wanted to hold and make love to my wife. Yet it didn't seem the right thing to do."

"Damn Jimmy, I don't know what to say." (Phone ringing)

"Hello Kevin, this is Brooklyn, is my husband there?"

"Yes he is, a little drunk but here. Hold on."

"It's your wife man so pull yourself together."

"Baby you okay, I was worried about you, its pass 2 a.m. and you aren't here. I miss you."

"I know baby, I got to drunk and decided to sit here at Kev's, for a while. I am on my way."

"Kevin, you know Brooklyn is up because she wants to make love."

"So what the hell is wrong with that Jim?"

"Nothing except it feels like I am losing her."

"Man, you better get it while you can. Soon you won't be getting any, not from her at least." *Jimmy leaves Kevin's place. Kevin is sitting on his white leather sofa with his pants down by his ankles.*

If this fool knocks again. I am not going to answer it. His wife calling sounding sexy on the phone "is Jimmy there". I swear he is stupid as hell, "Man my wife wants to make love and I am scared to lose her. Shit, Jimmy boy, I'd do her for you. I want to put this thing in her mouth. She got some pretty lips.

Picking up where he left off Kevin is stroking himself with thoughts of Jimmy's wife riding him. He climaxes and he sleeps in that position (hunched over) for the rest of the night.

Chapter 5

FEELING GUILTY

hen I open the door my wife was standing at the top of the steps, with the sexiest nightgown on. It hugs every curve, she has on glossy lipstick, her hair flowing, she's walking down the steps gracefully, the gown swaying at her hips, a split showing her thighs, pumps on showing her muscles with each step, she is pretty and sexy as hell, and I am a fool.

She hit the light switch and the music starts playing. I reached for the lights and the colors of the bulbs are soft with a yellowish and red tint. She walked right into my arms. She kissed me.

"Baby I miss you, we've been so busy, and we haven't had time to enjoy each other."

She took me by the hand. Lead me into our den, candles everywhere, fireplace lit with a soft yet sexy scent. There are bowls of strawberries and grapes, cantaloupes and watermelon including roses everywhere. A throw rug and pillows lay on the floor in front of the fireplace. She unbuttons my shirt with her teeth kissing me and teasing me. She dances for me, *strip for me*. I am hot so horny and yet so sad. I felt like a jackass at this very moment. She is so hot; she got my leg shaking as she is giving me a lap dance. She is shaking her ass so sexy and hot I could tape $1000.00 on each cheek and never have to touch her. She is crawling up between my legs biting me, teasing me; she takes me with experience and love. I stop her, I can't take it anymore she drives me crazy, she sends me into a frenzy. I lay her down and caress her body.

I kiss every curve suck every orifice, pull and bite and tease her entire body. We go to a place of bliss stars and magical themes until tears roll down our eyes in-sync. We lay in each other's arms listening to the music. I can feel her heart beat against my chest. Her breathing is fast and strong. I can hear her soft cry. I hold her tight. I hold her so tight I can't pull any closer. I hold on for dear life. Tears roll down my eyes. Right now it feels so good. I love and appreciate her so much. I could never want or need a better person, wife or lover. What hurt most of all she is my very best friend. I am crying because I never realize how much she meant to me until now. I realize right now because I feel I am about to lose her. I don't want to let her go. I pull her on top of me and cradle her in my arms. I kiss her and squeeze her.

"Jimmy I love you so much, baby you make me feel so good. I love the way you love me."

That did it. The guilt got to me.

I started crying right in front of her. I held on to her so close.

"Baby I love you too, with all my heart. You are so good to me and I have taken you for granted. I just want you to know that I do love you."

"I know you love me Jimmy. Baby I know."

We sit up in front of the fireplace. We sip some champagne and feed each other fruit. She throws in a porn tape, we watch, eat drink and smoke. We make love over and over and each time with more heat and intensity than the last until we clasped in each other's arms. The next morning she is up making breakfast naked.

"Baby where are the children?"

"Good morning babe, the children are at my parents until tonight. I want to spend some time with you. You don't have to work today, Do you?"

"No baby I don't. Even if I had to go into work I couldn't. The way you put on me last night I would have to call out."

We both laugh. I kiss her and hold her. I take her by the hand back to where we laid.

I finish breakfast. I feed her, bathe her and dress her. We hang out all day. We pick the children up. We go out to the movies and dinner. Children in the bed and here we are at it again. We have been going strong for a few weeks. No sign of Karen. I have not heard anything from her. I ask Brooklyn's parents to watch the children for us. I want to take Brooklyn on a trip to Cancun for at least 10 days. They agree. I make the plans with the help of my mother. I call her job make sure it's cool.

"Hey baby you won't believe the job gave me a 10 day vacation. Well they offered I accepted."

"Hey baby, I got 10 days off too, Brooklyn? Would you like to go Cancun this weekend?"

"Yeah, baby I think that is a well deserved vacation for both of us."

"Jimmy; after all these years and ups and downs in our marriage, I am still in love with you. My love for you, baby has never changed."

That was a stab in the heart. I look at her and smile.

"I feel the same sweetness in love until the day I die for no one but you."

My heart feels so heavy; I say a silent prayer for us:

Please God let her forgive me one more time.

I got to get Karen to get rid of this baby. I can't have Karen using this baby against me.

Man I am a straight selfish ass. I figure I can see a shrink when we get back from our vacation. Maybe they can help me tell my wife I fucked up again. In the mean time I am trying not to break down and tell her the truth. It is hard as hell. She seems so happy. The kids are happy. I am the reason why all the pain has been caused. Had I paid attention to my family we would have been happy, grooving along from the very start. When I look back at all the shit I've done to her, I can't imagine why in hell she'd put up with me. She doesn't need me financially. She makes enough to pay all the bills in one check. She'd kill me in alimony checks if she ever decided to divorce me. Hell with my track record they'd give her everything. No matter how I look at it, or try and switch it up, I loose. Fuck the material things. I would lose my best friend, my first love, my first lover, and my wife. When I think about my life, she has been there from the start of my man hood. I cannot believe how much of a fool I am.

"Jimmy, baby; are you okay?"

"Yeah, I was just thinking how we've been the last few weeks. We have been grooving on this high. I don't want it to change. Everything seems perfect don't you think?"

"No Jimmy everything isn't perfect, we got our issues, or at least you got some. However I love you. I decided that it was time for me to make a choice."

"What choice would that be Brooklyn?"

I thought she knew about Karen. I was scared to death… if I trip and she doesn't know. I will give myself away. If I play it cool, and let her talk, shit I don't know, I am just going to chill and see what this conversation is hitting for…

"To love you and stay committed to you, or hate you and divorce you. I decided to love you. I think going on this vacation will give us time to talk and start over fresh with no secrets no lies. Can we do that Jimmy?"

"Yeah baby we can."

That was something to go through. It is no secret that I am a horrible husband. Does she really know and she is giving me a chance to put it on the table? She even had a thought about divorcing me. Damn she is more ahead on this shit than I gave her credit for. Shit, damn fuck!!! She is going to force me to tell her and on vacation too. Damn if I don't tell her and the shit comes out when we return, she will leave me. I got to get at my man's about this, see what he thinks. Naw I have told Kevin too much already. I think he wants to fuck my wife. He sure as hell has been looking at our relationship. He has been looking at her a little too close for my liking. I'm tripping I know damn well Kevin knows better than to fuck, naw and Brooklyn would have told me if he hollered at her, well maybe or maybe not look at all the shit I put her through. She doesn't have to tell me a damn thing. I didn't tell her until I had to. Ok Jimmy you got to pull it together.

"Hey baby I am going to see my mom would you like to go?"

"Not this time Jimmy, I am going to see what I have to take on this trip, or do I need to go shopping for something new. Should I have to go shopping would you like to go with me?"

"Yeah babe, I'll go with you. I know I need some new clothes. You could buy yourself something new just for the hell of it. I'll be back in an hour or two, or call me when you're ready to go."

"Sure will do!"

I watch her go up the steps to our bedroom. There have been plenty of times Kevin has stood right here and watch my wife go up the steps to come and tell me he is here. My dick is getting hard from watching her ass bounce with each step so I know damn well his was too. Shit I want to go hit it right now. So I know he thinks about my wife. Well I hope to God he don't get any funny ideas. Shit she even knows his number; they could call each other at will. I'm tripping. I show her too much love for her to step out on me. Don't I? She shows me mad love and I step out on her. Well I'm going to ask her.

I walk in the room and she is on all fours and looking for something under the bed. I kneel down behind her.

"Can I have some of this?

"Any time you want it daddy. She turns around to face me."

"Brook do I satisfy you? Do I give you enough sex? She starts kissing me and pulling at my clothes. Baby do you hear me? Do we make love enough for you?"

"Jimmy; why you asking me questions like that? Our sex is satisfying for me. I love it that you still fine me sexy and want to make love in strange ways and strange hours. You sound guilty baby, you shouldn't ask questions that you can't answer."

"What you mean by that baby?"

"Jimmy will you just fuck me baby, don't spoil the moment okay?"

So I did what she asked.

"I'll be back soon. Okay Brooke."

"See you when you return."

My mom doesn't live that far from where we live maybe a 20 min drive. She actually lives closer to Brook's parents. The drive gives me time to think. My mom is my road dog and she gives me the best advice straight lace.

"Hey mom how you been?"

My mother is in the kitchen cooking as if she has kids home. I am her only child. And I think at times she forgets that I don't live here. She cooks for me every night. To make her feel good I come here for lunch every day.

"Hey Son, what's up?"

"Oh mom I got some serious problems and I don't know what to do. There is this woman I slept with who is pregnant and won't get rid of the baby. Mom I am so afraid of losing my wife. Brook wants us to come back from this vacation with all cards on the table no secrets and she had thought about divorce and I think if she finds out about Karen she'd leave me and I also think that Kevin wants to fuck my wife. I know he looks at her. I am un-sure if she'd tell me if he'd hit on her or not. Damn mom what should I do?"

I bust out in tears. "Mom I am afraid. Mom I am afraid."

My mother is looking at me; she walks up and hugs me.

"My poor son you are a foolish child. Why do you continue to sleep with these women without protection? Well I guess that is a useless question now. My suggestion is that you tell your wife the truth. Let her decide if she wants to be with you or not."

"What are you saying mom? You know she'll leave me."

"Son, you did not give that a thought when you were doing what you were doing!

I know you didn't come here for me to be sympathetic towards your foolishness! Jimmy if nothing else I will always be honest with you. When you're wrong and when your right I will be honest and I will always have your back no matter what as long as you're honest with me."

"Mom, I don't want to lose my wife. I don't want to lose my family."

"Well baby you should have thought about that before now, don't you think? Honey be honest with your wife and accept the fact that she could and just might leave you. Baby, she can also choose to stay, love has always found its way home."

"Mom I can't. I-"

"You need to face the fact that you fucked up son; you caused whatever happens from this point on. You should take responsibility for your own actions. Jimmy it will be all right. You will learn to be a better husband to your current wife or maybe a future wife."

"Future wife, I don't want another wife. I want the wife I got."

"Then my son act like it, show her how you feel even when she is not around.

Trust is everything in any relationship; it could make or break a relationship."

Driving back home I think about my moms, she has always been honest with me.

She has always given it to me straight she pulls no punches. I love her for that. I'm just going to be honest with Brook and tell her the truth about Karen. I pray she forgives me. I pray to God we can still be a family. Should things be any different at least she won't find out after the baby is born.

I'm riding by Karen's house; I need to find out what's up! I need to find out what this bitch is going to do about this kid she is carrying. I park a few houses down and walk up the street.

This is the first time I've been to Karen's house in the daytime. It is a decent home.

I ring the doorbell. A man answers the door. I was shocked. I got mad real mad, almost jealous, then I had to think. This is not what you want. Dude could tell I was heated.

"Are you here to see Karen? She isn't here. I am working on the house. She should be back in a few minutes."

"Naw that's ok, I'll catch up with her later, it isn't that important."

"Who should I say came by?"

"Don't worry about it man; I'll see her around. I was just driving through and thought to stop and say hi. It's no big deal thanks."

I can't believe I was feeling some type of way. I thought he was fucking her or something.

I got to get a grip on myself. As I start the engine she pulls up. She gets out of her car and gets into mine.

"What's up Jimmy baby, what do you want?"

"You know what I want, Karen. Are you keeping the baby or not?"

"I don't know Jimmy. I want a baby and I think you are a good father. I want my own family, my husband and child. I don't want a child by someone else's husband. I don't want a child by a man that doesn't want it. It's not fair to bring a child into this world knowing already that she or he won't know the father, or siblings.

I was being selfish the last time we spoke. I was strictly thinking about myself. Truthfully, I can't keep this baby; it just wouldn't be fair to it, or your wife or kids. I am too old for this type of bullshit. Jimmy I don't ever want to see you again. Please don't come by anymore. Please forget you ever met me. When you see me in public places don't speak ok. It's not that I don't love you. It's because I do. I don't want to share you anymore. I want my own man. Could you do me that favor?"

"Yes Karen; I'm very sorry. I am sorry that we got into this situation. I love my wife and I don't want to lose her. I should have been a better man. I didn't mean to cause you any pain. Can you forgive me?"

"You're forgiven Jimmy and good-bye."

She got out of the car and walked away. I watched her walk up to her home and she never looked back. She kept her head up high and walked right out of my life.

I don't know if Karen is telling the truth about getting an abortion. She didn't ask for money. I guess I should have offered. Anyway she seem like she was unsure and then very sure. One thing I admired about her, she knew what she wanted and didn't accept anything or anyone that was less. Brook would have cried and ran to her room and shut the door. Karen would challenge my man hood. I would have to make a choice. She would not have put up with all the kids I got. We would've been divorce by now and the bitch would have taken all my fucking money.

I guess I should tell my wife anyway. Then, maybe I shouldn't. What's the point of telling something that no longer exists? I won't fuck up anymore. No more cheating. I can't afford the risk of losing everything.

"Hey baby you ready? What are you doing lying down? I thought you wanted to go shopping."

"I'm tired Jimmy. Can we go another time?"

"Sure baby! Are you feeling all right? Come on, let's go upstairs and lay down together."

"The Kids are out back. I got to take them to my parents' house."

"I'll take them. I'll be back. Make sure you stay right there— Althea! Get your sister and brother and let's go. I am going to take you all to your grandmother's house."

"Yes Dad? You called?" I repeat myself, they still playing in the back yard

"Hey Daddy can we get some ice cream?" *little Brooklyn yells*

"Althea, get your sister and brother and let's go. I am going to take you all to your grandmother's house." *I repeat myself for the second time*

"Yes Dad you called?" she answers, so I repeat myself. The kids come running.

"Hey Daddy can we get some ice cream?" *Brooklyn asked again*

She is so pretty. She is the spitting imagine of me. She has my skin complexion, my hair, and eyes. She is taller than Althea was at that age. She'll be 3 in a few months. Little Jimmy is 1 and looks like his mother. He has girly features eyes, hair and complexion. He will with no doubt have a lot of women. I will teach him to be more respectful than his pops was.

The kids are in the car and strapped down. We buy ice cream and head over to see my in-laws.

"Hello Mr. Thomas. How have things been?"

"Everything is fine son. How are my grandchildren?"

"Hey pop-pop!" The kids scream in union as they run up and give him a big hug.

The kids and my father in law walk away, however Mrs. Thomas is standing in front of me with her hand on her hips. This clearly means she has something on her mind.

"Jimmy you know we love you and we have accepted all the flaws you have and you do have many. Now don't lie to me what is this shit I hear about some woman name Karen being pregnant from your ass?"

My mouth fell open and no words came out! I couldn't think of a defense fast enough.

"Close your mouth son", Mr. Thomas joined in, "now we have not spoken to our daughter yet. I wanted to speak with you and give you a chance to come clean and here is your chance son."

"Tell the truth son!"

"Baby he doesn't know how to tell the truth. This bastard isn't any good for our daughter!"

"Now, Mrs. Thomas *waited a minute*. I will not stand here and argue with the two of you. I would like to say something."

"Oh save it Jimmy. I am calling my daughter right now and tell her. You know if it wasn't for your carbon copy here. I would have told her already."

"Listen woman don't start your shit. I will talk to my son in-law man to man and you go tend to your grandchildren and leave the man things to me."

"Yeah, I bet you'll handle the man shit. So far you're doing about good as he is. The both of you are bastards."

"Look Son let's take a ride."

While riding to the park there were no words exchanged. No conversation. How in the hell did they find out? I guess my wife knows. Damn here I am acting as if I got away with some shit. It's about to blow up in my face. I don't know what to say to this man. It is his daughter that I have been running on. I know how I'd would feel if it had been Althea, Brooklyn, or Ayah I would most differently hurt someone without any questions. I wouldn't care if I'd known the man all his life. I guess that's how Mr. Thomas is feeling right now. Mrs. Thomas does obey her husband. She was really tripping on him. Brook never told me anything about him ever cheating on her mom. I guess she thought if I knew then I would expect her to accept the same from me. It tells a lot. I guess she put up with my shit, because her mother did. Maybe that's all she knows. Damn I sure got myself into some shit now. I must tell my wife now. I have no choice. It is better hearing it from me than her parents.

"Son", I know the shit is true. My wife first heard of this situation at the hairdressers where she and this Karen woman both go. She overheard Karen telling the hairdresser that she was pregnant with this guy's baby whom was married and refused to be a part of their lives. Then finally she said your name and my wife got so upset she went straight at the bitch's throat. The owner called me to come to get her before she had to call the cops on her. Look I guess you don't know but I have also cheated on my wife in the past.

I have two kids out there, two sons, which I have no contact with. My wife would not put up with it. She tried with my first son and he came around until he about 3-4 maybe 5 then his mother had another baby and that one was mine too. This meant I was still fucking the woman. Our relationship has never been the same. I want to be a part of my sons' life. However in order to keep the family I have I must let them go. Ok son, I have to be honest with you because I want you to be honest with me. I still see my sons. My wife doesn't know. My daughters do, because they need to know who their family is. That way there won't be any incest going on. Listen you don't owe my wife or me an explanations however you do owe my daughter one. She has put up with your shit for a long time Jimmy and you need to treat her better if you want to keep her. I am telling you from experience this one is going to change things between the two of you. I pray you two can work it out. I stuck through it all because I truly do love my wife and I deserve all the shit she is taking me through.

Now you son must decide if you can handle the bullshit Brooklyn might put you through. Do you love my daughter? Do you want to be with my daughter? Can you handle the shit that comes from a bitter woman? The bitterness you created?"

"Yes Sir, Mr. Thomas I do love your daughter. I am in-love with her. I don't know why I cheat. I can't put words to it. I spoke with Karen she said she is going to get an abortion and that's that, it's over."

"Son", I know why you cheat. It is exciting fun sneaking around like a kid. You're not a kid you are a grown ass man. You got daughters of your own. I'm sure you would kill any man fucking over them! Tell me I am wrong."

"No sir you are not wrong. I would absolutely kill any man messing over my daughters.

Well son, you need to make a decision now. That decision would be to come clean or not.

You see I cannot promise you my wife won't tell my daughter what you been up to. I can promise that I will try and keep her mouth shut until you two come back from your vacation. Then it is on you to make the right choices. Jimmy you also need to understand that I love my daughters just as much as you love yours. I know that I have done some pretty ugly things in my day. What goes around does come back to you. You see I am getting what I put out there. My daughter is hurting right now because of some nut ass nigger that is acting like her father was. And of course, the person hurting her is no-one other than you! I do indeed love you. I have known you all of your life. However, don't get if fucked up, I will with no question and no doubt kill your ass about mine. Now I want you to have a nice romantic trip and enjoy yourselves and you need to promise me you will take care of my daughter completely!"

"I promise you Mr. Thomas that I will take care of your daughter and I will tell her the truth about Karen and if she'll have me still, I will be the best husband that I can be."

"That's good son, that's good. Now here's your car, go on and have a good time.

"Oh Mr. Thomas can you do me a big favor?"

"Sure son, what can the old man do for you?"

"I would really appreciate if you never threaten me again!"

"Oh son, I wasn't threatening you, my dear child I was making you a promise and a promise to God that if any man hurt any child of mines he'd be as good as dead. It just so happens that I was being honest with you about my feelings and thoughts and I know that it would eat at me if I didn't tell you the truth. Otherwise you'd already been dead. Just do the right think son, don't worry about the rest."

Mr. Thomas drove off and left me standing there in a state of shock and anger. I wanted to shut his eyes right then right there. Who the fuck does he think he's talking to.

Then again I wouldn't even have given any man that much respect about my daughters.

I guess I deserve that shit. Well the big problem is my wife. I will have to tell her on vacation. I don't know if I should tell her in the beginning or the end. We will be here for two weeks and I don't want it to be mess up. Yet I don't want the shit to start soon as we get home either. Fuck it I'm going to tell her soon as we hit the resort.

I hope to God she forgives me. I hope more that Karen keeps her word and has that abortion. That would sure make it worst if there was another child to throw in her face.

Damn I just can't seem to get past stupid. What the fuck is my life turning into? Any man would love to have her as his own. I guess I just got greedy and now I got to pay for the shit. Wow this is some deep shit and I can't get mad at no one but myself.

Chapter 6

BETRAYED

*K*evin circles Jimmy's block for the third time.

Damn this dude hasn't been home in three hours. I have been watching his house all night. I want Brooklyn so bad I can taste her. I can smell her sex. I am tired of her fucking him. He can't satisfy her the way I can. I am tired of watching them fuck. The cameras I put in their house a couple months ago are getting boring. I want to be in the damn film. I am tired of watching her suck his dick. She should be sucking mine and riding me. I watched them fuck all week. She was dancing for that fool and kissing him and shit. He doesn't deserve that shit. I do.

Kevin pulls up in the drive way to their house

Look at this shit

He puts a DVD into his player and watches Brooklyn and Jimmy have sex in their bedroom.

Look like he doesn't know what he's doing. This dude doesn't know how to hit it right. Oh but look at her tits bounce… hmmm… I'm getting turned on by this shit.

Kevin pulls out his penis and starts stroking it.

Look at her now she is sucking my shit, oh Brooklyn that's how you do it baby. Damn look at that ass she is on all fours, this nigger don't know how to bang her out. Move over Jimmy boy let me show you how to hit it. You like it like that baby? Yea say daddy again. I like when you call me daddy.

Kevin sits in his car masturbates to the DVD.

Yea bounce that ass girl, yea like that, what? Jimmy, my name isn't Jimmy, why you calling out his name? Fuck this shit. I am going to settle this. I am your new man and you're going to be with me not this sucker. I can't take this anymore. I'm tired of you faking shit. I am going to give you what you need baby: a real man. Once I tell her about this dirty dick son of a bitch she'll be glad to have a real man like me that can give it to her the way she likes it.

Kevin takes the DVD out, puts it up, turns the car off and knocks on the door. Brooklyn answers.

"Hey Kevin, what's up? Jimmy isn't here."

"I know he's not here Brooklyn. I came by to see you."

"Well come on in. What is on your mind Kevin?"

"Listen! Brooklyn I don't know what or how to say this. I just think you are a beautiful woman and sexy as hell and you deserve a better man than the one you have."

"So you want to fuck me then, is that it Kevin?"

"Damn you are blunt girl..."

....

Jimmy pulls up in front of his house and sees Kevin's car parked in the driveway

Now I know damn well Kevin isn't at my house. I wonder what the fuck is his car doing parked in my driveway. This man knows when my ride isn't parked then I am not home.

He has no reason to be inside my house. I'm going to sit here, and see how long he'll be in there...

****

"No you are fucking crazy coming into my home telling me you want to fuck me. How the hell do you think you are better than my husband? You are supposed to be his friend. I can't believe you are doing this." Get the fuck out of my home and don't you ever come here again

Kevin grabs her by the arm.

"Well Brooklyn I'm not going anywhere and if you knew what I know then you'd probably be game to fuck me just to get back at him. Brooklyn I need you, I need to touch you and taste you. Please let me show you what real love is. Baby it would feel so good".

Kevin tries to kiss her. She slaps him.

"Kevin you know Jimmy would kill you if he ever thought you were up to this shit."

"Well fuck Jimmy. Brooklyn he continues to cheat on you, and you put up with it. You could have so much better you know he got that bitch Karen knocked up right and he's demanding that she have an abortion so you won't find out. Now you see he doesn't love you. I love you. I need you. I want you. I don't need those silly hoes to please me. I need you."

"Get your fucking hands off of me you dirty bastard. I could never love you. I could never be with you ever! So you think telling me that my husband has got another woman knocked up would make me sleep with you? Are you crazy? I would never for anything sleep with you. You ain't shit either. I am going to tell jimmy about this shit and right now you need to leave my home and never come back do you understand?"

He doesn't know how to handle you. He doesn't know how to please you like I could. I watched- *Brooklyn could see the rage in Kevin's eyes, black and cold. He is crazy. She tries to run he crabs her again. This time with a strong grip letting her know he is not playing with a full deck.*

"Bitch you are not going to tell Jimmy shit. We are going to make love and you're going to keep your mouth shut. Do you understand? I watch you make love to him. You sucked his dick. I watched you dance for him. I watched your lovely tit's bounce for him. I like the way your ass looks when I hit it from the back.

He drags her over to the TV and puts the DVD in.

You see bitch that's going to be us. You see the way he is kissing you I could do better than that. You see the way he's fucking you I could do better for you. It will be our secret and that's that!"

Brooklyn's eye's are big as golf balls as she watch the recording of her and Jimmy's personal life, she can't believe this fool taped them fucking and he has gone so far as to replace Jimmy with himself. How long has he been watching them?

"I've wanted you so bad ever since I laid eyes on you and I can't take it anymore. Your dumb ass husband is always telling me how good you are to him yet it isn't enough for him. I know you and I could be right for each other. I don't cheat and I make enough money to take care of us all. To be honest with you I am not worried about Jimmy killing me. He best is to be worried that I don't kill his ass-Now give me some of that good pussy."

"Get the fuck off of me Kevin."

He ripped her nightshirt exposing her naked body, she hit him, in the face, and he then threw her on to the floor choking her.

"I just want to love you Brooklyn, why does it have to be so hard."

He choked her until she passed out. Kevin pulls the rags of her nightgown off and sits back and looks at her.

....

Jimmy is still sitting in his car timing how long Kevin has been in his house alone with his wife.

Now about 15 minutes have gone by and this nigger hasn't come out yet.

Brook's car is also still in the driveway. I should go through the basement and check things out. I am afraid to. Afraid of what I might see.

****

Damn you are sexy and you are so beautiful. Why won't you let me love you?

Kissing her on her forehead, fondling her breast sucking them he pull his penis out.

I should just ram this dick right up your ass. You don't know when you got a good thing.

He sits back and looks at her.

Your body is crazy and its mine now.

Strokes himself

All you had to do was agree. I would have taken good care of you for life. I just wanted you to love me. Look how you fuck this nigger

He points to the TV.

He treats you so bad and you don't care. He treats you like dirt and you still love him. You're a stupid bitch.

He smacks her and then kisses her again and again. Her lip is busted and blood is running from her nose. He rubs his dick on her breast, stomach and face. He traces her lips. He starts to jerk off and squirts his semen on to her stomach. She starts to move. He grabs her throat.

"Don't move bitch. Don't move. I want you to be awake and feel this dick inside you. Baby I promise you'll love it. You'll love the way I can make you feel. Baby all you have to do is agree. I want you so bad baby, please just say it. Say you want me...Tell me you want me Brooklyn say it!"

"You fucking bastard just kill me. I have never and will never want your ass."

He punches her in the face and she is out again.

****

...Damn. This nigga has been in my house for 20 mins. Something isn't right. I open the basement door as quiet as possible. I could hear Kevin yelling and talking crazy to my wife.

"I just want us to be together."

I run up the steps and Kevin is kneeling over my wife. This nigger is about to rape my wife. Blood is coming from her face, and her face is swollen. He has her legs spread a part and he is about to enter her. I kicked him in the face he is out cold. He hit his head on the ceramic coffee table. Kick him in the ribs a couple of times.

I call 911, the ambulance and police are on their way. I should blow this bastards face off. All in due time, first I must take care of my wife.

"Baby" I start to cry, "Damn baby are you okay?"

She isn't moving. Blood is coming from her nose and her mouth. Semen is all over her stomach and breasts. I turn around and kick this nigga in his dick.

"You mother fucker I am going to kill you."

I pick my wife up and cover her and hold her. I notice the TV, a recording of me and Brook making love. What the fuck, this nigger has been recording of us. What the hell is going on? You sick fucking bastard. I am going to kill you for this. You are one dead man.

The police come in and with the paramedic they cuff this motherfucker and then put his ass on the stretcher another ambulance is on the way. They are working on my wife. Putting needles in her arm they put her on the stretcher and now we are on our way to the hospital. Damn this shit is crazy. I knew he wanted my wife. I just didn't want to believe it. I never thought in a million years he would take it. He me told too. He told me in so many words he wanted my wife. He is a jealous mother-fucker. This fool has tapes of me and my wife. He has been watching us fuck. Oh my God what have I done? This is some off the wall bull-shit. I can't get this shit out of my thoughts. He was trying to take the pussy. This Negro has gone over the deep end. Well I am jumping with him right off the deep end and I'll see that mutha-fucker in Hell. I am going to straight nut out on this nigger. In college this dude didn't have many friends. He had a few chicken heads though. When I think back; once he was with them or fuck them, they never came back. They never called again. There was this one chick Jena, she was so afraid of him. I just thought she was scared of men. I remember a few times walking in on them fucking and this dude just kept at it like I was not there. He didn't try and cover the girl's body or nothing. He just kept banging her like they were alone. I thought she was a freak and liked that shit. Now, when I look back in retrospect that girl was scared to death. Damn I was dumb. I could have helped her.

"My; poor baby girl. You sick bastard. I can't believe you did this to mine. You will pay for this."

She could have given it up but she didn't. She'd rather die then give it up. That's my baby and I don't deserve her.

The doctors at the emergency room said her jaw was broken. They had to wire her mouth shut. She said she wasn't raped; there were no signs of forced entry. Her face is bruised and swollen. This is my entire fault. I let some crazy nigger into my home and into my life and this is what I get: my wife beat up and damn near raped. God what the hell have I done. My mom is right. I need to be responsible for my actions. I fucked up this time and bad. I hope she forgives me.

I sit watching her sleep, she moves around a little. I should call her parents. I should call her sister. I really don't know what to do. I could wait until she wakes up and let her decide. Maybe she doesn't want them to know what happened to her. By the time we get back from vacation her bruises will be gone and her jaw, hopefully, will be healed.

The police walk in.

"My wife and I want to press charges on this guy."

"We need to ask a few questions. First sir did you know this man. The reason I am asking, is this man was let into your home."

"Yes sir I do know this man, he was my best friend."

The cop looked at me and shook his head.

"You never know son who will turn their backs on you. I never let any of my male friends around my woman and I sure don't talk about the bedroom action. There is always a jealous fool lurking around waiting for that door to open up and take what you got."

"I thought he was attracted to my wife. I never would have believed in a million years that he would do this. He beat and attempted to rape my wife. Is this man going to jail?"

"Wife's going to press charges huh?"

"Yes sir she is!"

"How do you know? Have you asked her? Have you talked with her about what her intentions are?"

"I know my wife sir and she will press charges against this motherfucker."

"Well, your wife has to say the word and the charges will be filed."

"We will hold him until she wakes up for attempted rape and attempted murder charges."

"I thought the state picks this type of shit up."

"The state does, but this case isn't easy. She let the man in your house. We don't know if it was consensual or attempted rape."

"What? Are you serious? Do you really think a woman with a broken jaw and a busted face appears to want sex from her attacker?"

"The assault could have been someone else. He could have come to her aid."

"My wife had his semen all over her. Didn't you see the sexual recordings of my wife and I this man made?"

"We have the DVD sir; however you two could have made that tape. She could have been watching it with him. The three of you could have been watching it together and someone got a little jealous or a little rough. Who knows?"

"Didn't you perform a rape kit on her?"

"I am sorry sir, according to the law the incident is speculations and until your wife wakes up it will not go any farther. We will hold him as a suspect in an attempted rape and murder charge. He can also press charges on you for assault."

"You are joking?"

"No sir I am not. You kicked the man in the face. His jaw is also broke."

"The motherfucker is lucky I didn't kill him right then."

"Now sir that would be a threat and I am an officer of the law. What you say to me can and will be used in a court of law."

"I am a witness that this man was assaulting my wife."

"You could also be a jealous husband going off the deep end so let's wait and see where this leads when your wife wakes up okay?"

The detective walks out.

I sit there looking like a fool. My wife is lying here fucked up. I can't believe this shit.

This nigger could get away with this shit. Well if the law doesn't get at him. I will. I am going to kill this motherfucker. He will pay for this shit.

Brooklyn starts to wake up. The medication must be wearing off. Damn what am I going to say to her?

"Jimmy, Jimmy oh god. He was going to rape me Jimmy-"

She mumbles her words I can barely make out what she is saying. She is talking through clinched teeth.

"Its okay babe, it's ok".

Tears are running down her face. She is shaking.

I cry with her.

"Baby I am so sorry."

She looks at me and pushes me away. She curls up into a knot and pulls the blanket up to her face and cries really hard. I try and comfort her. I try and hold her. She doesn't give in to me. She doesn't want me touching her. I don't know what to do. I didn't know Kevin would do this. I didn't know that he would go this far. I didn't know the man was a psychopath. I call my mom. I can't take the pressure anymore. I tell her over the phone what happened. She flips. And she is on her way to the hospital.

I meet her in the parking lot. She is crying. I can't stand to see my mother cry.

"This is your entire fault jimmy."

"What? Mom I didn't know he would do this."

"I know you didn't know Kevin was an ass. You let this man know all your business. You let this man know all about your wife and how little love and respect you had for her. You sat in your car while this man was beating your wife.

Son you have been so focus on just you that you don't see how your actions are affecting everyone around you. It is affecting every one that loves you and the people you love".

"You're blaming me for Kevin's actions."

"No I am not. I am blaming you for your actions. Your actions gave this man idea that he could step in and have your wife. Her loyalty to you is what got her into trouble and almost killed. The worst part is you don't have the same value for her as she does for you.

"That is not true mom and I love my wife. I do value her."

"You need to think about that son. Do you really value your wife?"

"Mom what kind of question is that?"

"Son it is a question you need to answer and not for me but for your family especially your wife."

I break down right there in front of her. I am on my knees. I am praying and crying and falling apart all at once.

"My wife my beautiful wife, please god please forgive me."

My mother tries to console me but her arms are not what I need at this time. I need my wife. I need her to know that with no doubt I love her. I love her with all my heart. I leave my mother in the parking lot and I go back to see Brooklyn. I love her so much. God please forgive me. Please don't let this be the end of my marriage. I can't live without her. Oh my God I am nothing without my wife.

That night the doctors wired Brooklyn's mouth closed. She had to change her diet to all liquid. She had to write anything she wanted to say down on a tablet.

I question her about telling her parents and she wrote that she would tell them herself. She wanted to wait until we came back from vacation. Thank God she still wanted to go with me. Thank God she didn't entirely push me away. She didn't want me to touch her. She still let me sit with her and be around her.

I called her job and extended her vacation for another 6 weeks. I also took family leave from my job to take care of her. I called the travel agent and we extended the vacation from two weeks to 30 days. Her parents agreed to watch the kids. They were a little confused to why they haven't talk to their daughter. However her sisters assured them that she was ok and they also promised not to tell their parents.

She didn't want me to touch her sexually. I slept on the chair in our room.

She didn't want to speak about Karen and the possible child that might or might not be out there.

The doctors said that Brooklyn was in good health and it could take up to six to eight weeks for her jaw to heal. We board the plane to Cancun and arrived at our resort without incident or much conversation.

Chapter 7

THERE SHALL BE NO OTHER

T he first week it seemed like I was there alone. She didn't have much to say and she didn't want me to touch her at all.

We went about our days separately for another week. I was feeling some type of way. I complied with what she wanted because I felt like I should. It was hard though, not to be self-centered.

And this situation certainly gave me the chance to see how much of a self-centered bastard I'd become.

The third week presented itself and Brook could speak a bit better. I had just come back from the gym. I walked into our room it was dark, there were candles lit. The air carried a hint of vanilla and brown sugar, soft and sexy. I got excited to think my wife wanted me again.

I stood in front of the bed. There was this man lying in his boxers in my motherfucking bed. THEN Brook brings her ass out of the bathroom with a robe on. I am about to lose it. I just stood there in disbelief.

I turned and walked out. I am standing in the hallway. I can't believe she would cheat on me. Brook was a virgin and I was her first and only. That was my pussy! No one had ever had that but me. Now I'm sharing. She is giving my shit out. I should kill her and the nigger she with. Damn this is some shit. I guess I deserve it. I guess that's how she felt when I stepped out on her. I don't give a fuck. She should have stepped up then. I am not going to take this shit. She'll do it again. I know it. She'll be fucking different nigga's whenever she feels like it. Then I'll be the stupid husband sitting at home like she was the stupid wife!

I guess this is what you call checkmate. This is some shit to have thrown back in your face. This is some cold-hearted nasty bitch shit I didn't think she had in her. She isn't any different from the next bitch. I guess that's how I made her feel. I have been standing out here for 20 mins and this nigger hasn't come out yet. I wonder if she sucked his dick. The question is have I ever eaten another bitches pussy? Hell yea and she loves to suck dick. I have never had to ask her and when I unbutton my pants she got my dick in her mouth like chomp, chomp! There's never no question and no doubt when I want my dick sucked I just got to think it, drop my pants and it is done. Hell if I stand in front of her too long she is pulling and tugging at my pants trying to get at my dick. So I know she is sucking this niggers shit. I should blow her fucking brains out or break the other fucking jaw. Oh shit her jaw is broken (ha- ha) she can't suck that nigger's shit.

The room door is opening. This nigger walks out fixing his pants. Fuck this shit I am stepping to this motherfucker about mine.

"Yo my man, that's my wife you were fucking."

Right and left. The nigger dips it. He hits me one to the body. He throws a left I dip that shit. Connect with my right then left. Upper cut to the chin. He's falling and so am I. I get smacked in the back of the head.

****

It's dark. My head is spinning. I wake up in a dungeon called jail.

"What the fuck!!" I scream to the top of my lungs. "Brooklyn," I yell my wife name.

"Shut up you dumb fuck."

One of the guards is slamming his stick against the cage. I spent the night in that shit hole. Brooklyn bails me out the next afternoon.

We are in our hotel.

"What the fuck was that. You think it's cool to fuck another man in my face. I could have killed that nigger and you for that matter."

"Fuck you Jimmy. You never gave a damn how I felt. How you made me feel. My fucking mouth is wired shut. I can barely talk."

"You know Brook I am sorry that I caused you a lot of pain but you didn't have to get back at me like that."

"Nigga I know you don't want sympathy from me. I have forgiven you and forgiven you over and over again and four kids later. You got two kids the same age as our child. You make me sick Jimmy and I don't give a flying fuck how you feel. Do you understand that I don't care anymore? I should have left your ass in that jail because that is where you belong. You belong caged up like the animal you are."

"Fuck you Brook, you ain't the woman I thought you where and be mindful about that mouth of yours. You will not speak to me like that."

She is walking around the room in her panties and her tits are bouncing around. She is so sexy. I have never seen her so angry before and the shit is turning me on. She also was being a bitch and I want to punch her in the face. I don't hit woman but she is pushing my buttons.

"I can't believe this motherfucker is standing here as if this is my fault. Who does he think he is? I can't believe he said that shit. I am not the woman he thought I was." She is talking to herself, throwing her hands up in the air. "Well fuck you Jimmy. You're not the man I fell in love with. You're not worth shit. You run around on me and the kids with whores and you don't have any respect for us. Fuck you and your pride. You're that nigga that no good; shittin ass nigga that believes his own shit doesn't stink. I can't believe I stayed with your worthless ass Nigga."

That did it. I grab her by the arm and threw her on the bed. You want me to treat you like a bitch and a whore? I am going show you how bitches and whores are treated. I grab both of her wrists and hold her hands above her head with one hand. She is bounce and squirming around making her titties bounce. I started biting her on the cheek and bit her on her chest. I ripped the panties off. I'm grabbing and pulling on her nipples with my teeth.

****

He grabs me threw on the bed and held my hands above my head. He's biting me on my face and my chest. He's grabbing and pulling on my nipples with his teeth. I am mad but the shit feels good.

I pull my dick out,

He pulls his dick out, I pretend like I don't want it. I move around until he grabs my throat.

She's fighting me; I grab her by the throat.

"Open your legs bitch."

"Fuck no. Get the hell off of me."

I got her legs open; I'm about to tear this pussy up. I'm going to show her what it's like and how whores gets fucked.

I ram my dick inside her; I am trying to fuck her as hard as I possibly can. She is moaning and her pussy is more wet than usual. She likes this shit.

He is throwing that dick like he should've a long time ago.

For every thrust I give she gives it back to me. She's working that body like a whore.

"Fuck me you bastard fuck me like you will never get this pussy again."

I'm not holding her down anymore. I am holding myself up. She got her legs wrapped around my waist. She is throwing that pussy like no other. It is so wet and juicy

She releases her legs and flips over and is on all fours.

I flip over and backed this ass up on him. I lift myself up on my feet as to squat. I am throwing this pussy at him.

"Do you like this nigga? Is this the way you want it? Go head daddy and slap this ass."

She is backing that thang up. Oh my god she is talking dirty to me. She is asking me if I like this pussy. She is asking me to smack that ass.

I smack it (lightly)

"Mmm work it baby."

"Smack it again and call me your bitch."

I smack it again.

"You bitch. You pretty bitch."

I am going to teach this motherfucker a lesson he will never forget. I tell him to lie down and let me ride that thing.

"Lay down daddy and let me ride this big dick."

She is asking me to lie down.

I squat on the dick and I'm moving it slowly up and down

She is riding the hell out this dick. She moving slow at first up and down now giving me deep strokes and moving her hips in a circle this shit is good as hell.

I am riding this dick like a champion. I get up to go into the bathroom I got something for his ass.

She gets up and goes into the bathroom, I am laying here with my dick hard as a rock. If she had not gotten up I would have bust in a matter of mins. What the hell is gotten to Brook she never fucks me like this. Show you got to get a little manly on a bitch to make them act right. Ah here she comes strolling across the floor. She got something behind her. It is probably some freak shit. I close my eyes I can't wait to feel this shit. It probably some shit she learned here.

The nasty motherfucker got his eyes closed. This shit is going to be funny. I pull out my whip and start beating his ass, one across the dick and across his stomach. I just keep lashing at his ass.

"You dirty motherfucker, did you think you would get away with fucking on me. Nigga if you ever fuck another bitch I will kill yo ass. Nigga don't you ever get this shit fucked up."

This nigga is trying to get away. Slash across the face. Every time I hit his ass his skin jumps open.

Ah; ah Brook stop baby stop

I felt a sting and cut on my dick.

"Ah! Shit!"

I open my eyes this fool got a whip and she is whipping my ass. I try and run for the bathroom she slashes me again. She is talking mad crazy shit.

"Ah!"

"No nigga don't beg me now nigga. I begged you for years about this nut ass shit you do. You got nigga's wanting to rape me and other bitches having babies. Naw nigga you want this ass beating. This is the shit you looking for. This is the shit you and nigga's like you need. You want to act like a buck then get beat like one."

Slash, slash, and slash over and over again. Blood is everywhere trails of it leading to the bathroom where this motherfucker is hiding.

Damn I got cuts everywhere. Blood is all over the place. My dick is throbbing and bleeding and half my body is all fucked up. I call to my wife.

"I am sorry Brook. I never meant to hurt you. I am so sorry. Please forgive me."

I am sobbing.

I hear my husband begging from the bathroom door. My heart wants to forgive him. Then again as I think about it only half my heart wants to forgive him. I sit at the close bathroom door and listen to him sob like a kid. I start crying myself. He opens the bathroom door. Blood is everywhere. I grab some towels and ice out of the small refrigerator and start covering the cuts with ice and cold water. The bleeding stops and I patch him up. He doesn't want to go to the hospital. We stayed together in the bed and held each other.

"Brook, can you forgive me? I can't live my life without you. The shit you just did, I guess I deserve that. Baby please can we start fresh?"

"Jimmy I am going to try and forgive you. With everything that's happened, and the other baby and Kevin trying to rape me; it will be hard. These things are happening to me because I am married to you. I will try and forgive you ok?"

I am holding my wife in my arms right now and half of me want to choke the shit out of her. This bitch beat my ass with a whip. My dick is swollen twice its normal size. I can't believe this woman did this shit to me. I guess I deserve it. I have been an ungrateful self-centered bastard most of our marriage. All I know is that I love this woman so much that I'd rather her beat my ass then leave me. She is all I know.

I should tie this bitch up and beat her ass with a whip and show how that shit feels.

"Brook, wake up. You sleep baby?"

"No I'm not sleep."

"My dick is hurting real bad. I don't want to go to the hospital here. I might need to cut this trip short. I don't know that I can take this pain."

"Baby, do you want one of my pain pills?"

"Yeah, maybe that will work. This pill won't kill me right?"

"No. Do you think I would kill you?"

"Brook you beat my ass with a whip. I am shocked. You got me to my weakest point and then took advantage of it, which was cold."

"Jimmy look at me. Listen to my voice. Count the children you have and count the kids we have. Look at the bruises on my body and tell me how warm your love is."

"You got a good point and again I am sorry. I guess sorry isn't good enough. Baby I am going to change. I promise I am going to change. I have changed here with in my heart. I don't ever want to lose you. But I don't know what to do about this girl Karen. She claims she is going to have an abortion. She wants an abortion because I am not going to be a part of this kids life should she keep it."

"Well why would you do that? Really you would ignore you own flesh and blood. You do know you would lose respect from your other children."

"Why would you say that? I don't want this baby."

"What makes this child different than the other children you have? Just because you don't want it doesn't give you the right to ignore it. You should have thought about that before you lay down with this woman raw. You should have never slept with this woman because you are a married man. When you decided that wasn't a good enough reason not to sleep with her, you gave up the right to talk about children you don't want. You should have worn protection then you wouldn't have gotten caught up with this bullshit here. You shouldn't take it out on the child.

Jimmy I accepted your children because I love you. I allow your children in my home because it's not their fault you're an ass-hole. I am not trying to insult you or belittle you. You seem to think about no-one but yourself. Like no one is troubled by your actions but you. You have other lives you're responsible for. Your actions hurt other people. Especially the ones you claim to love. This child is a product of your actions and you're willing to turn your back on it just to save face with me. In my opinion you should have never fucked this girl and none of this would be an issue. I should have been more important to you. It's too late now to worry about how I will feel or the action I might take."

"Brook, you will accept this child. You are telling me you will accept this kid and not throw it in my face? You won't leave me over this? You're willing to make this marriage work."

"I am not telling you anything about me Jimmy. I am not saying that I will or won't do anything. I am saying it's too late to be concerned about me now. I didn't cross your mind while you were making this baby. I shouldn't cross you mind now that he or she is on its way to greet you. Baby your expectation of me shouldn't be any higher than the respect you give me. The question is do you want this marriage to work? Are you willing to work at this marriage? Do you think you've hurt me enough? Do you think I have been hurt enough behind the shit you do? Do we fuck enough? Don't I please you? What makes you run off to other women? Why would you fuck another woman without protection? Like really baby I don't understand."

"Brooklyn, baby, you are great in bed, no woman compares to the love we make. I really can't explain it to you. I just never considered any of the things you are saying. I guess I have been selfish and self-centered. Baby don't cry, please don't cry. My intentions where never to hurt you or have another person hurt you. Brooklyn this is going to sound stupid and senseless. I was just having fun in the beginning. Then I became greedy. I wanted what I wanted with no thought of any consequences. It had nothing to do with how much I love you or the respect I have for you.

Brook I love you with all my heart. You are my first love. The only woman I do love. I guess I haven't showed you much respect at all. Things will change I promise things will change baby. I am going to change. I still don't want this baby. I don't want any more kids. We got enough."

"You don't want the one I am carrying? You want me to get an abortion?"

"You're pregnant? I thought the doctor said something about you not being able to have anymore."

"I don't remember having that conversation with anyone Jimmy. How could you know that?"

"Baby you're my wife. No I don't want you to get an abortion. It's going to be alright baby. That pill you gave me is making me sleepy baby. Can we talk more when I am fully alert?"

"Sure Jimmy when you wake up."

I am watching my husband breathe. He is a handsome man. Jimmy is sexy and fine as hell. I know why women want him. He has a great career and drives a Benz and it's paid for. His house is paid for. His money is long and he's not stingy with it. He is a good provider. His investments have a multiple return. He really doesn't have to work another day in his life. I too have the same profile. If I leave his ass he will have to pay me half of whatever he has. I don't really want to leave him. All this shit I've been through with this man. I don't see the point in leaving him. I don't know how to live without him.

This man has been a part of my life all my life and he was my first kiss and my only lover. Everything I have he owns half of it, even my children.

Speaking of babies, I don't know why I told this nigger I was pregnant I am not keeping this baby. I thought about it and I don't want it. I want my children that I already have to grow up and live good lives and I need to stop being in Jimmy's shadow and live my life.

I kiss my husband on the lips, He pulls me close. He moans. No doubt of pain. He has an erection, but he isn't using that thing this week. It's all busted up. There's nothing wrong with his hands and lips. He will give me service. He wraps his arms around me and caresses my body a little and we both sleep. I woke up in a heavy sweat. What if this baby is Kevin's oh my GOD. I start crying and shaking. Jimmy woke up.

"What's wrong baby and why are you crying?"

"Nothing, I do not know why I am crying. I just feel sad."

I could not tell him what I had dreamed. We were having enough problems besides I am not keeping it now for sure.

A few days later Jimmy was still in bed. He had a temp. I tried to wake him.

After a few slaps he came around.

"Baby I think you should go back to the states and go to the emergency room. I think your wounds are infected."

I didn't want to tell him that his dick was about to fall off nor did I want to go with him. One part of me wishes it would fall off. I might be tired of him and it anyway. He looked down at himself.

"You know Brook this is your entire fault. If my shit is fucked up it will be on your hands. You had no right doing that crazy ass shit you did. Man if I lose my, you know what; I am not going to say it. I'm gonna ride with this shit. You just need to know that if something happens to me you should go to jail for this shit."

"Yeah," You should go as well Jimmy. All the shit you did to me was painful too and I don't want to have a pity shit party. You need to go home and get your dick checked out. My mouth is damn near wired shut because of your lose dick. That thing needs beating because you cannot seem to control it. I think it has a mind of its own and thinks independently from your other brain. Do me a favor baby, and tell that motherfucker I would not give a rat's asses if he did fall off."

"You bitch, you saying you don't give a shit if my dick falls off?"

"I am not telling *you* that. I'm saying it to your dick. I would never tell you that baby. I love you and all you've done for me. However that dirty dick bastard is something I can do without."

"Bitch you have lost your mind. My dick and I are one in the same."

"Oh really, so your dick don't have a mind of his own. You're telling me that you pulled your dick out each and every time you were out there fucking? Your dick didn't just fall into some pussy. You actually put it there! Then you Jimmy it is best you go home and take care of yourself and when I get there please be gone out of my home."

"Bitch, that's my home too. Okay wait a min. baby this is going too far. I am not leaving my house. We can work through all of this."

"We can do what? We can work through what? You weren't thinking about me when you were working in all that pussy you found. Now, we don't have to work through anything. What you need to work on is how to keep yourself healthy. Jimmy I don't know how I feel, all I know is you should go home and go to the emergency room and then get your shit and leave and give me space to think and to sort things out. I do suggest you go home today because you look real bad."

I look down at myself. I do look bad. I don't feel good.

"Baby," Could you call and change my flight."

****

"Jimmy your flight leaves in an hour. I have your things all packed and ready to go. You'll be leaving on a medical flight that way you get half of the trip cost back."

"I love you so much Brook. Thank you. I really do love you."

"Well, you always say that. Too bad you rarely showed it. Anyway, the hotel is going to escort you to the airport and make sure you get on the plane safely and there is a nurse on board and a doctor at stand by. Please don't fuck the nurse and take care."

I watch Jimmy get into the car with hotel staff and drive off. I am sitting here alone and this is the first time my husband has been this far away from me since college. Oh well, might as well as make the best of it and have fun.

The phone rings and its Jimmy telling me they kept him in the hospital. His wounds are infected, which, of course, is no surprise to me. He is on IV antibiotics and will be there for a week.

Chapter 8

LONELY

The phone rings again and it is our travel host.

"I wanted to invite you to our festival it starts a nine, come dressed to impress darling there are a lot of handsome men here."

"I will be there thanks for the invite".

What will I wear? Oh I have this short little red number with the back out and a v cut in the front past the navel. My abs will show. Uhm, Jimmy would *die*. Oh well.

Looking good girl and feeling sexy. (Looking at the reflection in the mirror)

The party is in the lounge and alongside the beach; some had bathing suits on and some were dressed as I am. There is slow reggae music playing. I walk across the lounge floor over to the bar. It seems funny-before now, I would have never dressed this sexy without my man beside me. Men and women were staring at me. I walk towards the beach and someone reaches out and grabs my hand. I turned around to see a high school class mate Jeff Henderson, what a surprise and comfort. I had felt really alone. Jeff was a nerdy kid back in school. He had nerdy friends and was into nerdy things. No one bothered him, he was always found at the weight room and right now he is still built very nice. I really didn't pay much attention to him back then. He was tall his upper body was really big from lifting yet his lower body look like twigs. He looked funny to me. I never saw him with a girl. I saw him in the weight room or in court yard with his big bottle cap glasses and book or with his nerdy friends. Today he is fine and everything is symmetrical like it should be.

"Jeff is that you?"

"Hello Brooklyn, how are you doing? Where is your other half?"

"Oh Jimmy had to cut his trip short, he'd gotten sick and needed to leave."

"I can't believe you guys are still together. That's a beautiful thing. How many children do you two have?"

"Well Jeff, Jimmy has about six and one on the way. I have three and none on the way. I really don't want to talk about my relationship."

"Oh, okay. I understand I do understand."

"Where is your wife?"

"Oh Brooklyn my wife died in a car accident a few years ago and I just haven't found any one to meet my standards."

"Your standards, you have standards that a woman needs to meet? What are you doing taking applications?"

"Well that is a good term for it. I guess so. Listen baby if you don't stand for something you will fall for anything. Listen, I am a good man. I don't do the cheat thing and I don't want a slut for a wife. I need to be careful who I bring home. I like serious relationships."

"Okay Jeff. You've never had a fling?"

"Oh of course I have. Haven't you?"

"No."

"Okay Brooklyn. The last time I heard something about you, you and Jim were getting married and you two already had a baby girl."

"Yep, Jeff that's true."

"I'm not saying it right. Let me ask you this, you haven't been with anyone else but Jim?

I felt stupid for the first time in my life. Hearing someone say it made me feel stupid. I drop my head. No Jeff only Jim."

"Why do you have your head down? Why you are all teary eyed. Brooklyn, are you embarrassed?"

"Yes. I am embarrassed."

Jeff orders two glasses of white wine.

"Is wine okay for you?"

"Yes I guess so."

"Let's sit on the beach and talk."

He nods for the waiter to follow us with a little table and our drinks.

"Is there anything else you need Mr. Henderson?"

"Yes sir, keep the glasses full."

And then he stared at me from head to toe. He put his hand up to his chin as if he was thinking.

"Oh yes. And my lady friend will need an extra large beach towel to sit on and a little something to cover her where her dress will stop once she lays down. Thanks."

I am impressed with the respect he is given, the waiter returns with the things Jeff asked for. Jeff laid the towel out. It is big enough for the two of us to wrap up in. The table is sitting behind us. We are looking at the ocean

It's warm. The air is warm and a full moon is shining above the blue water. The scene is picture perfect; it really would be if it were Jimmy and me. He takes my hand and helps me down onto the towel. He takes my shoes off. He sits next to me.

"Brooklyn why would you be embarrassed about being a true honest woman?"

"Why, I feel foolish. Look at all the children he has. I know you have heard about this Jeff. I just feel like I gave the best years of my life to this man that never appreciated me at all."

"Okay and you're embarrassed? You have nothing to be embarrassed about. You are a beautiful and wonderful person and that is something to be proud of baby."

"You don't understand Jeff, my jaw is fractured I was beat up by one of his friends and I think he raped me after he knocked me out. Jimmy said he didn't. I have been so confused about my life. I have been on such an emotional rollercoaster ride."

"I know how you feel. I was working late as usual and I decided that it would be nice for my wife and me to go for a late night scroll in the park. Brooklyn she was eight and half months pregnant with our child. I thought the walk would be good for her. A police chase was in progress when she got off the express way and a cruiser hit her head on and killed her. The doctors tried to save my son and failed. I had to bury them both. The first time I held my son was the last time I saw him. My wife was so mangled that it left horrible visions. When I think of her I see her crushed up. I still can't get the scene out of my thoughts."

We were both crying and holding each other like we needed each other.

The waiter kept our glasses full as Jeff had asked. I swear he was standing right next to us. Every time I took a sip my glass was refilled. The waiter came up to Jeff.

"Sir the bar is closing would you like for me to send a bottle of wine to your room sir?"

"Yes that would be a good idea."

Did I hear him right?

"Jeff, the bar is closing? What time is it? Where did all the people go?"

"Baby it is three am."

"Damn we have been out here that long; running off at the mouth."

"No we have been out here communicating. I have never expressed myself like this to anyone. I have been keeping inside for so long. Thank you for listening Brook."

He grabs my hand and I stumble, he wraps his arms around my waist and carries me to the lounge floor.

"Can you stand now?"

"I think so."

I stumble a little more. He holds me close.

"Brook I think you're drunk."

"I don't feel drunk."

"I am going to take you to your room okay? You should be okay once you lay down for a while."

"I don't want to go back to my room Jeff. I have never been alone."

"You are serious. Okay my room it will be."

His room is like an apartment. He has a living room with two sofas, a chair, and a flat screen. He has a small kitchen, an old fashioned soak tub, and a stand up shower. His bed is oval shape and turns around in circles. White and gold are the colors of his bedroom, Beautiful.

We are sitting on the sofa. He puts soft music on and sits next to me.

I lay in his arms. I feel so safe here. I look at him.

"Jeff, I feel so alone even though I am married I feel so alone and lost. I feel like my little fairytale world is falling apart and I don't know how to hold on and I don't know if I want to hold on. I am afraid to let go and I am afraid to stay. I asked Jimmy to move out. I don't have anyone to talk to. All these years there were never any one for me to talk to."

I just let it all out I was shaking and crying I couldn't stop crying. When I open my eyes Jeff is crying almost as hard as I am. He had no one either. His wife and son were dead and he felt guilty. He'd been carrying this around for a while with no one to talk to. Poor, baby. He is a good man.

I don't know what came over me. I kiss him. He looks surprised but he kisses me back.

He is on top of me. His kiss is soft and sensual. He pulls back. He takes me by the hand and I stumble almost falling down. He catches me. We walk to the shower and he turns it on. He takes my dress off and my breasts are exposed. He's looking at them. He licks his lips and moans.

"Uhm you are beautiful."

He pulls me into the shower he begins to wash my hair and my entire body. The water is perfect and his hands are soft and my body wants him. He isn't naked. He has his shorts on. I touch his chest and caress him. I kiss his neck. I can feel his man hood growing in his shorts. He moans;

"Brook uhm, this is one of those very hard things I must do."

He turns me around rises me off and steps out of the shower. He grabs a towel and gently dries me off from head to toe. I feel so at peace and he has me so excited. He picks me up and carries me to bed. He leaves the room and returns with a different pair of shorts on and some wine. We drink. We are sitting in silence. You can hear the waves outside. His slide door is open a little, enough for the breeze to come through. Candles are lit. He climbs in bed next to me. He pulls me into his arms.

"Brook"

"Yes Jeff?"

I look up at him and he kisses me.

"I want you so bad girl, but this isn't the right time. You are so pure and innocent and Jimmy is a damn fool."

He is breathing heavy and his heart beat is fast. He throws the covers back and pulls away and then he kisses my neck and traces the outline of my body with his two fingers.

"When I--you will have to be available to be my woman and I don't share. He sits back down and lays my head on his chest and holds me so tight and we slept. The next morning I wake up to breakfast in bed and a tall glass of water.

"Good morning."

"Good morning Jeff. I hope I wasn't too much to handle last night. We drank a lot of wine. Did we, you know?"

"Oh trust me Brook you would have remembered that."

"You are something Jeff for a--well you're something."

"I am what?"

"You're a gentle giant and it is so nice to be with someone that won't take advantage of me. My friend, your kind is hard to find."

We ate laughed at ourselves in our drunken stupor

"Brook I meant what I said last night. I want to be with you. I want you to be my woman. I will not ever share you with another man."

"Jeff we haven't seen each other since high school."

"Brook I always had a crush on you. I was unsure of myself. I didn't know if you would accept me. We are different. Now, wow have you grown up. I really have a crush on you. I am not saying it would work. I am saying I would like to try. I am saying should your marriage not work. I'll be around. However, please don't use me. It is okay just to be friends. However, I don't fuck my friends. You can't kiss on me and rub your ass up against me and tease me and shit. There has got to be a balance. I don't want to just fuck you. You are a good woman and you deserve the world at your feet. I can't put the world at your feet darling, but I can make you feel like you're standing on top of it."

"You are so sweet Jeff. In high school you were just nerdy. Now you are handsome as hell for -- well, you know?"

"What do you mean?"

I am playing Jeff. I meant for an ex-nerd you are very handsome and very sexy. I don't play games. Hell I don't know how. I do respect what you're saying and I thank you for having the upmost respect for me. It was all yours last night and I am thankful you were gentlemen."

We both laugh.

"You'd be easy to love Jeff. I really need a friend right now. I am so confused. I have not thought about another relationship in my life. I don't want you to be under the impression I would ever leave Jimmy. We are going through some things right now and I need to sort things out. I need to take some time off from being in Jimmy's shadow and work on me. Do I make sense to you?"

"Yes you do Brook, and I thank you for your honesty. I think it would be a pleasure to be your friend. I am glad you were up front with me. Hey you go back to your room and get cleaned up and maybe we can do some sightseeing. This is a beautiful country we need to explore it and have some fun."

"Sounds good to me I'll call your room when I am prepared to go."

"Hey Brook, no sexy clothes ok. I am not telling you how to dress, it's just that you were kind revealing yourself and I am a man. I can see and I do look."

"Got you Jeff, I understand and I apologize."

It has been two weeks already. We are sitting on the couch at Jeff's penthouse suite.

"Jeff I have had so much fun being around you. You make me feel so important and loved."

"You make me feel wanted Brook. I love how you adapt to my needs."

"Oh I haven't adapted to all your needs, Jeff not yet."

"Brook, Can I kiss you."

"Yes."

He moves closer and kisses me lightly and then I can't help myself. I grab him and kiss him. His lips touch mine and I explore his mouth with my tongue

I sit on his lap as we continue to kiss. I can feel his manhood rise. If I don't stop now I won't be able to stop. I am a married woman. I don't feel married. I don't feel loved or respected by Jimmy. His hands are exploring my body and my temperature is rising. I am moaning under his touches. He pulls my shirt off and we are going at it. He kisses my entire body lighting up places I didn't know existed, with his lips. Then he stops.

"Baby, I can't make love to you Brook. I want to so bad. I just can't be with you like this.

I respect you too much. I can't have you break my heart when you go back to your husband. I don't know that I would be able to handle that. You would need to get a divorce or at least file for one. Then I will ravage your entire body baby and give you all that you can dream of. I am falling in love with you and I don't know if that's a good thing."

"Jeff, I have strong feelings for you too. I am scared and happy and sad all at the same time. I don't know what came over me. I didn't know that I could feel this way for another man. I wish things were different. I want you bad too. I want you a part of my life. I have to go home soon and return to my everyday life. I have to deal with Jimmy and what we could have left if anything but at the same time I don't want to give you up. I don't want to let you go. I need you Jeff in my life. You are a beautiful person. Baby I need the love you can give me."

"Then Brook I suggest you get rid of your baggage. I will stay in contact with you after this trip. I won't wait long Brook for you to make up your mind. I haven't felt this way since my wife and son died. Please don't string me along. Please don't use me. Please don't hurt me."

I looked up into his face and he is crying and showing me so much emotion. My heart went out to him. I knew then this is the man I should have been with all along. I cuddle next to him and we hold each other. We kiss now and then. He caresses my breast now and then. This man has me on fire. We lay this way for hours and then it is time to go home.

We take the same flight back home together. I have one of my sisters pick me up from the airport. I watch Jeff get into his limo. Damn this dude has money, power and a big heart.

I am thinking about how Jeff treated me. He was courteous and very thoughtful of my feelings and very sure of his own. He is a patient man and he loves to be loved. Oh God how am I going get my life together. This man could give me the world. Yet my heart belongs to Jimmy and he is all I know. Maybe it is time to get to know someone else.

Maybe it is time to give another man a chance to love me. This love I have with Jimmy doesn't feel good anymore. It hasn't felt good in a long time. I don't know if I still love him or if I am just used to being with him. The ride home is an hour long and it gives me time to think about some things. My life is a whirlwind. I don't know how I ended up here. I have never been alone. I don't really want Jimmy around. I am scared of Jeff, I guess the unknown. I am unsure. I got these kids and they love their father so much. My heart is beating so fast. I just can't trust him anymore. He got a truck load of children that are not mine. Every time I see his child it's a slap in the face how little respect he had for me. How little he really loved me or how important his family is. Well I don't know what I am doing with Jeff; I do know what I will not do with Jimmy. I don't want to be with him anymore.

Chapter 9

KEVIN

How did I end up here, on a hospital bed and chained to it? What the fuck is going on. My jaw is hurting bad. A police officer walks in.

"Sir you are being charged with attempted rape and attempted murder and assault and a slew of other charges."

It all came back to me. Brooklyn and I were about to make love when her stupid husband came home. They took my ass down to the jail after they wired my mouth shut. This fool broke my jaw. He is jealous. Brooklyn wanted me. She likes it rough. I stayed in that hell hole for almost a month, eating slop for days in and days out. They are going to pay for that shit. I couldn't even call anyone because I couldn't talk. If Jimmy thinks this shit is over, he is crazy. Don't no-one hurt me like this and gets away with it. I am going to kill this fool. I will have my way with his wife.

I don't know why she is pretending to be with him. She knows I can do better by her than he ever could. I can see us living in his house and me playing with his kids. They will call me daddy and I am going to enjoy playing with his wife. That woman has a nice body on her. I don't see the reason he had to cheat in the first place, but never-the-less, it's my turn now. Jimmy has got to go.

I got off on some technical bull-shit. These fools violated my civil rights. They searched my house without a warrant and could not use any of it against me. They really don't have a case. I was a lucky ass. I could be facing 10 years right now. I had all kinds of tapes of them fucking all over the house. I did it because I wanted to know what kind of woman I got.

I wanted to know what she likes and what she dislikes. I wanted to know what makes her feel good and what makes her cry. She is a good woman and God has spoken to me. He made her for me. This fool is in the way. I must find a way to get rid of him. I have been watching the house and no one has been home for weeks. I've seen her sisters go in and out of the house a few times. I've seen her parents with our children go in and out a few times. Up until last week no one was there. Then this fool is home alone. I wonder if she left his simple ass. I wonder where she went. Damn this fool is living in our house all by himself. We can't be happy because this dude wants to be selfish.

I am sitting in front of their house now. I am across the street in the bushes waiting for the perfect time and opportunity to strike.

Oh shit, it's a car pulling up into the drive way. That's my baby getting out.

What the hell, she's going back to this dude. Baby you don't have to worry much longer. I will get him out of your life for good.

It's too many people there now. I am going to find me a friend and lay up for a while. "I'll be back, Jimmy boy."

My car is two miles away. I parked in front of one of my friend's house so the cops wouldn't be suspicions. I know they are trying to follow me. Those detectives cannot do anything to me. How is it possible that this rooky cop failed to obtain a search warrant? These fools walked up into my home, no warrant in hand and searched my shit. The cops were talking mad shit too.

"You're going down for this one Kevin. We've done our research we know you had those cameras put in that house. We know you were hiding out in their bedroom, you perverted bastard. We got you here on tape filming yourself standing in the closet watching them have sex while you masturbated. You're going down for this dude. You beat the day-lights out of that young lady and she don't want you. You're a sick son-of-a-bitch. What is this Kevin some altered personality disorder? How many people live in that sick brain of yours?"

Another detective asks more stupid questions.

"What in the world would make you sit on their roof watching them as they came and went? Man, answer this for me; why would you tape yourself peeking through their window and jerking off? What the hell is going on?

You're not a bad looking dude you have your own business. You're making good money. Hell you're making twice my salary. Why would you want to throw it all away on someone that has no interest in you? Kevin this woman will never be interested in you."

"Look, fuck you cop. Man you have no idea. She wants me. She needs a good man like me. That fucking husband of hers does not know how to treat her."

"Kevin and you think beating the senses out her is better?"

"I didn't do that. I don't know how that happened. I just wanted to show her that I could love her and take care of her and our children, I mean her children. I can provide all she needs."

"Dude she is a married. You and Jimmy are friends. How could you lose control like that? How could rape a person?"

"I didn't rape her. She wanted it. She likes it like that. She likes to be beat up and then we fuck, Drama."

The officer grabs Kevin by the collar.

"You are one crazy bastard."

Kevin's lawyer walks in.

"Keep your hands off my client, or I'll be force to file a police brutality suit against you and the department. You have no documented evidence against my client. Your rooky cop entered in his house without a search warrant. You have no reason to hold him. Let's go Kevin; you don't have to put up with this kind of treatment."

"You dirty mother fuckers, Yah, trying to keep a nigger down." *Kevin spoke in anger and a loud voice.*

The lawyer pulled Kevin into a private room. "Look Mr. Cobbs you are dealing with some serious charges. I need for you to tell me the truth about this situation here with Mrs. Williams and her husband. The information I received states that you were Mr. William's friend, is this true"?

"Yeah, Jimmy and I were friends, until he started telling me stories of how he was cheating on his wife. This shit went on for years, since college man, and I just got tired of hearing it. He got a good woman at home. You know Mr. Kelly he has been with this woman since high school and she has not been with another man outside of him ever. She is a virgin in my eyes."

"Mr. Cobbs your wondering eye has got you in some deep water, now I see that it is true you have put cameras all over their home. According to the police report you had over 30 cameras installed into their home. They have over a hundred films that you taped of their personal life. You have more than half of Mrs. Williams alone. I need to know why."

"Mr. Kelly, I fell in love with this woman over the years and I wanted to get to know her better. I knew she would not give me much attention; she was so devoted to her husband. I needed to know what she liked what she dislikes, what made her laugh what made her cry. I wanted to know what made her feel good and I needed to know how to love her. I know what she needs Mr. Kelly and I plan on giving it to her. Have you seen those tapes? She's beautiful, a shining star, she is a good mother and good wife and she is hard working and very intelligent, and to ice it all off she is sexy as hell, her body is gorgeous. You cannot tell she has any children. Uhm I am getting excited thinking about her. I need her."

"Mr. Cobbs get a hold of your-self. I am your lawyer so you won't have to worry about confidentiality however you need to watch what you say. You sound sick. This woman is married and it does not matter how bad her marriage is, she has not made any advancement towards you and you should stay the hell away from her. You are not permitted to go anywhere close to her or her family and that includes her husband. Now you have a good chance of getting off here. Lucky for you all the evidence is worthless due to the stupid rooky cop. However don't involve yourself in anymore mishaps; you might not be this lucky next time. You know that man has every right to kill you. Had you done this to my wife, you'd be dead now. Hell I need to check my best friend. This has sure taught me a lesson about friendship. You are a scary individual Mr. Cobbs; you are every man's nightmare."

This lawyer was talking crazy.

"Whatever; just do what you gotta do Mr. Kelly to get this shit off my back. I will take care of the other matters. Everybody will see in the end that I am not the problem, Jimmy Williams is the problem, he should have kept his dick in his pants and his wife would not be looking at me."

"Mr. Cobbs have you ever thought about getting help for your delusional problems. Sir you are not dealing with the here and now correctly. You are not living in reality here sir. This could be another reason you walk. You are insane. I will call you and set a date and time we will meet and discuss your defense and of course my fee. This case is going to trial; the District attorney is taking it to court. I also want you to be evaluated by a professional. I think you really have problems."

"Whatever you want man, just do your job. I got to go and handle something. This situation is about to get ugly. I have to prepare for the worst and I don't have time to waste talking to you about my family. Call me and I will meet you were ever you chose. I will bring a check with me."

"Mr. Cobb, stay away from that family. Do not have any contact with them for any reason. Do not go anywhere near them. The farther you keep the distance, the better your chances of getting off, and not going to jail for the rest of your life. Do you understand what I am saying sir, Do you understand you are not allowed to go anywhere near them at all."

"Yeah man I hear what you're saying. No cop has told me that I can't speak to my woman. No judge has told me that I can't go see my wife. There is no law stating that because I had a little love spat with my wife that I can't go and make-up with her and continue on with our lives."

"Mr. Cobbs every cop in this county has told you within the last 36 hours, and if they didn't I am telling you, wake up and see this shit for what it is. You are violating these people's rights, and you are going to jail or the graveyard if you don't leave them alone. When you go into a market and notice them there, leave what you have and come back at another time. Do not be seen anywhere around them and sir that is an order. Now you have the right to disagree with my suggestion and should you want to uphold that right, than I have another suggestion for you."

"Kelly now what would that be, my man, you seem to want to control my every move."

"No, I do not want to control your every move, just this one, and the advice is should you not be able to comply, you can get yourself another lawyer."

"I hear you sir, and I promise you will not receive any negative reports.

Man I guess Mr. Kelly was right. I won't let anyone see me. It doesn't make much sense to get caught in some bullshit. I'd be in jail and my family will be left all alone. I gonna watch and see how my baby Brook is holding up. I am standing across from their house. Thank God this old lady across from them is too old to cut down her bushes. This fool Jimmy has been home alone for a couple of days by himself. I had the perfect opportunity to take his ass out, that changed when I saw my baby get out of the car and go into the house. I wonder if she is going to forgive him for all this bull-shit. She better not give my pussy away to this fool. Man if she fucks this Negro, I am going to be mad as hell. I do not get down with the cheating game. I'd have to kill her. I have invested a lot into making this relationship happen.

Chapter 10

HOME

Brooklyn *is entering the house; Jimmy is sitting at the kitchen table.* The house smells good. He cleaned up the mess that was made during my home invasion. I stand at the door looking at my husband. Half of my heart loves him and the other half is so hurt by him. He stands up and walks over to me.

"I have missed you so much. I hope you can find it in your heart to forgive me. I have changed Brook; being here alone in this empty house by myself has showed me what would happen if I don't change. Coming home to a mess and all the shit I saw the last-time I was here almost killed me.

The things Kevin did to you are my fault, I brought him into our home and I gave him reasons to violate my family, I am so sorry baby. I can't live without you Brook. I just can't live without you and I feel like such a fool."

"Jimmy I love you too, and I married you for better or worse and this is indeed the worse I have endured. I am going to try and forgive you. It will take some time. I look over at the TV and flashes of that day come rushing through my head. I start to shake and tears start falling. He was going to rape me Jimmy; He had these tapes of us making love. He has watched our ever move. I am afraid. What if he comes back? He thinks I should be his wife. He is crazy Jimmy, he's crazy. What am I going to do when you go to work? What is going to happen when the kids and I are here alone?"

My wife comes in and I try and explain the emptiness I felt while she was away. I had the time to reflect on my life without her and it is not something I want to live through. I will never cheat on her again. She is standing at the door as if she is scared to come inside the house. She starts crying and remembering the shit Kevin did to her. Man if I had not come in when I did I don't know what he would have done to her. He could have raped her. I also could have prevented what he did do to her. I could have come in earlier, God forbid she finds out I was sitting outside tripping while this fool was in here beating the shit out of her. I could have kept my dick in my pants and just be a husband to her. She is shaking and telling me she is afraid to be here alone. I pull her close and hold her.

"I am so sorry baby. I am so sorry."

I have to hold her up. Damn this fool has my wife terrified to be in her own home.

"We can sell the house baby and move somewhere else. We can rent it out immediately and buy another house if you want to. I would do anything to make you feel better."

I take her upstairs and undress her and put her in our bed and I start to walk away. I had intended on going into the basement. I didn't think she wanted me to touch her.

"Jimmy where you going? Please don't leave me alone, I am so afraid."

I get in bed with her and hold her. I know she has not forgiven me.

"Please hold me Jimmy."

Her cell phone rings. She answers it. It's a man's voice on the other end. What the fuck, I don't say anything because I really don't have a right to and I don't want to give her a reason to bring up all the shit I've done. This shit is getting deep and I hope I can handle whatever is to come my way.

Jimmy takes me upstairs and puts me to bed, I do miss him, I also do not want to be anywhere in this house alone. He starts to walk away. I ask him to stay. I am laying in his arms when the cell rings and its Jeff. I answer.

"Hey sweetheart, Hello my sunshine, I called to see that you got in safe. I enjoyed our time together. I also would like to say, should we become nothing but closer friends. I appreciate the time and care you gave while we were together. I really needed that listening ear. I hope everything goes the way you want it to Brook and I wish you the best in your marriage. Just remember my love if it does not work out I am here for you. You may have to find me, but I am here. My heart is yours baby and I do love you. Please don't say anything and good night."

He hung up the phone. I am just so overwhelmed with all these feelings. I know Jimmy could here that it was a man's voice on the phone. I felt no need to explain anything to him and to my surprise he did not ask. He held me closer as if I was slipping away. He made love to me like he has never did before, so much passion and so intense. He made me know that he loved me and he made me remember why I fell so deep in love with this man.

It is seven am and I can smell coffee. I rise up and go down stairs into the kitchen. I need to make sure it was Jimmy cooking breakfast and not Kevin. That man is a sick person. I have this strange feeling he is still watching us. I think he will try again. This time I will be prepared for him.

"Baby you're making breakfast? This is so sweet to wake up to!"

"I wanted to bring breakfast to you in bed baby. I wanted to show you that I can take care of you, the way you deserve to be taken care of. Go and get back into bed, will you do that for me Brook?"

I run back upstairs and take my clothes off and get back into bed. About 15 minutes later he is bringing me breakfast and we talk.

"Babe I know you feel confused about staying with me. You deserve better treatment from your husband. I can't take back or change what has been done to you; however I want to show you that I will be the husband you deserve. I will be the friend you need. I pray you can forgive me one day."

"Jimmy, I just feel so violated and lost, I hear what you're saying but I don't know if you're right. I am confused. I know you love me but what kind of love is it? I don't know if I need what you have to offer. I have been loyal to you, loved you and only you and you have been the only man that has been between my legs. You got babies across the globe and I have accepted each and every one of them. Are you sorry because you got caught? What if Kevin hadn't done what he did, like serious if he wasn't crazy would I have ever found out about Karen and her unborn child?"

"I was going to tell you on vacation, your parents made sure I'd tell you."

"What? My mother knows about this shit, Oh shit, and my dad as well, how the hell did they find out?"

"Your mom and Karen go to the same salon and she overheard Karen telling the hairdresser and figured the woman was talking about me, seeing that she said my name."

"When was this Jimmy?"

"They confronted me the day you were attacked. Remember that day I took the kids over so we could spend some time together? That's the day your pop put me in my place. I had planned on telling you everything. Then this motherfucker decided to take you. You know I'm going to kill this nigger right?"

"See Jimmy, this is the shit you don't seem to get."

"What babe? I'm trying to be honest, please don't get mad all over again."

"Jimmy I am the joke of the county. Are you serious? You don't see how everyone knows about you and your dirty secret and your dumb ass wife is the last to know? And now you're crazy ass friend wanted to fuck me and take me for him-self. Wow Jimmy you don't see what it really is. Everywhere I go, someone will be whispering about us, how you treat me. Hell, how you've been treating me! People already talk about how many babies you got on me, now the psycho friend and another whore are added to the story. You really expect me to forget all this shit that you've done all these years and just get on with us?"

"Babe I don't expect you to forget, I want another chance to make it right. I want to be the man you need, I want to be the man you love and take care of you, love you. Babe you know I love you and would never want to lose you."

"You should have thought about that shit before Karen and before Kevin. You should have been able to look at me and see that I was fed up with the bull shit. That one more thing and I'd pack my shit and leave."

I sat there listening to my wife go back and forth with her emotions and confusion has set into her mind. She is right; she has never cheated on me. I am the only man she has ever been with. I am the father of her children. We have a life that most people die trying to get it. I fucked up big time and I don't know how to fix it. I put my arms around her and attempt to hold her. I kiss on her shoulders, she pushes me away at first, I guess because she is bitterly angry, then she gives in and lets me hold her and touch her, we sit in silence and I can tell it won't be long before there is a change in her.

I'm sitting here in Jimmy's arms and he's doing all the things I used to enjoy, he's cooked for me, fed me, he is caressing my breast as we watch TV, showing me so much love and affection and I feel like the shit is fake. This nigga stepped out on me so many times with so many different women and now there is a nut case on the loose that he used to call "friend", trying to take over my life. Sitting here in bed with my husband as he caresses my body would have sent the old me into frenzy. I would have been ready to explode with passion. And he controlled me with it too, with my own bless it passion.

As I look back, I realize that every time he had stepped out with another bitch and got her knocked up, he'd spend the week sexing me up and making me feel like he was the greatest man in the world, then drop a bomb on me, oh baby I did it again, like a dumb ass I say "oh you got another you to look at." Just that easy he'd go on with his day. Come home and crawl in the bed with me and sex me up another week thinking that solved all my worriers with his dick. It did, I was so hooked on this fine ass man with the greatest sex in the world that I must have figured I couldn't get anyone else.

Right now he is sucking on my breast and it's hard to ignore because the nigga knows my body inside and out. I want to give in and let him make love to me, yet I don't want him to get the impression that fucking me every night and day will make me stay here with him. It won't, I am going to start dating other men and see what is out there. I don't know if I could sleep with another man yet, well hell I could've slept with Jeff if he'd let me. Outside of that I have not been that close to a man to see if I would or could.

Now this nigga got his head between my legs and he is good at it. I can feel my body respond although my mind doesn't want to. I'm slowly giving in because I can't help it. He has mastered every inch of my sexual being, he can make me have an orgasm so fast and continue to have them over and over again. I figure I'd be him for a while, see how he can handle it. Go ahead poppy do that, right there, and I'm going to step outside to see if another nigga can compare.

I want to see if he has the greatest sex game or is it that he is the only man I've been with so there is nothing to compare him to. Hmm, I am going to spread my wings and find out.

I swear I hear someone in the house, this nigga is sleep and I am scared to death its Kevin's ass up in here watching our every move. The police claimed they removed all the cameras and I hope my husband changed all the locks and the security system was set up by the time I got back from vacation. However I don't trust this fool. This morning I am going to buy a gun and learn how to use it. I refuse to be a victim in my own home. My children are living between my parent's house and his mother's that not fair to them. I really can't take this shit much longer. Something or someone has got to give.

I'm at the gun shop; I have no idea what I'm looking at. The sales woman comes up to me,

"Can I help you with something?"

"Yes, I want to buy a gun."

"Do you know what kind of gun you want?"

"No, I know nothing about guns. I just want something to protect myself with."

"Ok, maybe a .22, it's small and easy to handle and it has no kick back."

"Well I want something that will put holes through bricks, something that will lay a big person down."

"Well we have a .45 or a 380, both are great hand guns and they will stop any person you shot."

"Ok, well I will take the .45 and bullets."

"Alright then, you must fill out this form, it will give you a license to carry it. You cannot take the gun with you until the license comes back and the permit."

"How long does that take?"

"You should be able to pick up your gun in two to three weeks. I will call you and let you know that it is ok to come and pick up."

"Do you know of a gun range nearby?"

"Yes, I will give you a business card. There are the phone numbers and address on the back of the card along with the directions on how to get there. I think you need to be prepared for whatever happens in today's world. I know about your home invasion and wish you the best of luck dear."

Before I could respond to her she had walked quickly away and I felt like my whole life was on display for the world to see. Damn.

To my surprise Jimmy was home when I got there.

"Hey babe how was your day." *he said as I walked in, some shit he must have heard off the Cosby show. He never talk like that, I didn't reply, just simple waved and went upstairs. I think I am growing bitter. Everywhere I go, everyone looks at me and whispers, even at my fucking job. This is a bit more than better or for worse. This shit is the worst; it's foolish. There is just no way to feel right about this. I get paranoid when I'm in any part of this house alone. I feel like I'm being watched by someone, and at any time this fool will come rushing out the closet and kill me.*

I don't like being forced to be up under him either. Well I'm going to the shooting range tomorrow and learn how to defend myself against this monster and hopefully he doesn't come back at all. However should he get the notation to do so, I will put him where he belongs.

I'm trying my best to be the man I think she wants. Hell I have no idea what the fuck she wants in a man because I have been only focusing on what I want in every women I come in contact with. This shit is hard as hell. I greet her when she comes in; she waves as if I'm some neighbor in the yard. Are you fucking kidding me? This is some serious nut ass shit. I cook for her, I clean for her, and I sit in the house for her. I haven't seen my other children because I'm so worried that this nut as nigger will come beat the shit out her ass. I understand what her pops meant now; can I handle what will come after the truth? I know I don't want to lose my wife, but have I already lost her? Her whole demeanor is different. I just don't know what to do at all.

Chapter 11

KEVIN IS BACK

I have been watching this house for two days and they haven't left at the same time yet. The cops took all the cameras out of the house and I need to put them back or least one in the bedroom and one in the living room. I need to see what's going on in there. I want to know what this fool is up to. Why my wife is still with this nut. Baby I know you are waiting for me to rescue you from this fool. I'm trying baby, It takes planning and decision making skills to make sure everything falls into place; I promise you Brooklyn this motherfucker will never bother you again.

Finally everyone has gone; I haven't seen the children in a while. I wonder what that is all about. It doesn't matter. They will come home to a new daddy, a better daddy, and they will be happy. Life with me will be more of a heaven instead of the hell they are in with Jimmy. He has enough children to deal with outside of this house he don't deserve the ones that live here. We will have more children. Damn it was hard getting into here. This nigga done went and put in new windows new locks and a steal door. I had to finagle some shit in order to get in this mother fucker. Alright a camera is set up within the TV.

I'll be able see what they are doing as a fake ass family. Now I do think I should put one in the basement? This is where that fool does all his thinking so I can see were his mind is at. This is really taking a long time to accomplish. This shit was easier the first time around, well I didn't have to do it all in one day and I had access to the house because they trusted me, I guess I fucked that up. Damn my game was off, I got so overwhelmed by her beauty, that I needed to be with her and lost patience and focus. Now I got to start this shit all over again. I should've been more patient and when I get you into my arms, my dear, you will see the patience I have and I will apologize to you for being so hasty in my ways. I'm sure you will forgive me. Hell you better, you forgave this bastard for all the wrong he's done. Damn this dude must be going through some changes. The basement is messy, looks like he has been living down here. That's right baby don't put up with his shit any longer. There are beer bottles all over the place, glasses here and there, plates of eaten food, soda cans. Wow man clean after your-self and you think my baby is a maid? Fuck outta here, soon my man you will be out of this house. I wonder if this nigga got some smoky smoke.

Ah, jackpot lets smoke a blunt maybe two, what's this? Yo this fool is doing cocaine now, wow times seem hard dude. I haven't did this since college, oh well lets reminisce down old school lane together my friend, ex-friend. I know he got some blunts around here, shit this place is so disorganized you can't find a damn thing, let's stop and think like Jimmy boy. Where would he have put the blunt wraps?

Kevin is sitting in Jimmy's and Brooklyn's house smoking cocaine laced blunt watching TV and reminiscing on the day he forced his way into their home. He is sitting in Jimmy's chair with his feet up, totally relaxed as if he is really home. Over an hour goes by and he is still sitting in the same spot. He is astronomically high from the drugs and getting deeper into his own thoughts. Kevin is unable to separate reality from delusions.

Opening the refrigerator, there is a couple of open bottles of beer; I'm thirsty this will do, I got something for this Negro. Drink this; this is what I think of you. I want you to know when you're sipping on my urine; you'll soon understand where our friendship has gone and my ex friend, its gone straight to hell. You put me in this situation and gave me no choice but to act on it. You showed me what type of man your wife needs and as I looked in the mirror. I see that I am that man, all that you could not be. I am going to provide and defend her up to my dying day.

I didn't want to hurt our friendship in the process however you just won't move on with your life and you don't love her enough to let her have a fulfilling life with a man that can appreciate her for her worth. Now for the bedroom; let's see where do I want the camera? This thing needs to be position where I can see everything but not where they can see it. In the door jam of the master bathroom I can see both in the bathroom and the bedroom. This is where she has her thoughts and moments where she talks to herself about what she wants.

She stands in the mirror and talks about how she feels about all his cheating and other fucking children that she is forced to accept because she loves him. That is what she believes, that she's forced. I'm here now babe and there will be no more heartache. No more pain. I am here to provide and profess my undying love for you. You are what every man dreams of as a boy visualizing his future. You are what every husband needs: a woman that will be there through the good, bad, and ugly. Our ugly will be the college bills for the kids. Our ugly will be the dirty dishes the kids leave behind and we have to clean up. Your heart will always be at peace and filled with love.

Kevin smells the bed sheets and decided to lie in their bed. Brooklyn I can smell you. I need you so bad baby, I gotta have you soon. The cops say rape or attempted rape. I would never rape you baby. I want you to give it to me freely and willingly and know that you will not be disappointed.

Kevin is takes his clothes off and starts to masturbate from his wild and crazed thoughts. He images himself being the husband and man of the house. He rubs the sheets against his man hood and proceeds to climax without thought or hesitation. He gets up and takes a shower and redresses. He hears the door open and shut.

What was that? Damn I have been here to long? I didn't realize the time had gone by so fast. I've been here for five hours... oh shit... someone is in the house what am I going to do? I'm not prepared for this confrontation yet. Damn I gotta hide. I guess it's the closet. I hope it's not Jimmy but if it is I got my nine on me and it will be what it be.

Chapter 12

DOING ME

've decided that life is too short and precious to leave it up to chance. I can't live a false life with Jimmy. I love him so much and I thought I married the man of my dreams. My dreams never consisted of infidelity, children out of wedlock, and a crazed friend that thinks I'm his wife. My dreams never consisted of tear-filled nights and lonely days because my man was off doing someone else. He is not at fault alone because I chose to keep a blind eye to the bullshit.

Well not anymore. I refuse to stay where I'm not appreciated, where I'm not loved and respected. I know Jimmy loves me; however, I need to learn how to love me more. I need to learn how to respect myself and know my self-worth. I need to understand who I am and what I want. I have catered to this man for so many years, it's beyond foolishness or stupidity.

In life it's okay to be a young fool, not knowing what to do, or allowing shit to repeatedly happen to you is how we learn. The process of becoming an adult usually happens with mistakes made however I refused to be an old fool for this man. I think I'm going to get all dolled up leave the children with their racket ass father and call Jeff and let him know that I am ready to be his woman. I am ready for a life filled with love for me. I need and want the love I give, I must have the respect and loyalty I give and of course be treated as royalty.

I'm meeting Jeff downtown, there is this restaurant that I've never been to and I'm eager to go. The crazy thing is Jimmy is always downtown and it's possible that we'd run into each other. Well maybe not because he'll have the kids then who knows with him. I'm at a point where I really don't give a damn who it affects. No one especially Jimmy didn't give a damn how I felt and it's about me and my happiness. Abraham Lincoln put it best. "We are all as happy as we choose to be" Make sense. I choose to be happy with another man because the one I'm with makes me fucking sick.

I'm sitting here in my bedroom and the bed is all messed up and there is cum stains everywhere I know damn well this motherfucker didn't have a bitch in my bed. He has gone too far. "Fuck you Jimmy" I scream. You are about to see my ass walk off in the sunset with a better man. I hear this man downstairs so I yell to him. "I'm not going out for a while to meet some friends so your kids are on you and they have not eaten dinner nor are they bathed or prepared for bed. He yells back, "what I have somewhere to go as well you can't put this all on me." his voice trails off as I slam the door, fuck you pussy I think to myself.

The hours and years I've spent taking care of your kids while you're out making babies with someone else. Clean and cooking bathing and feeding them while your ass sat up entertaining the next bitch and you absolutely didn't give a flying fuck about what I had to do or wanted. Handle it motherfucker or do what you do best run to your mother. Swing on her left tit and have your kids swing on the right one, just get it done player.

The restaurant is more beautiful than I imagined. There are candlelit tables soft music playing it's a lover's dream, the tables are far apart from one another and that gives a lot of privacy to be a little close. Jeff is already there looking handsome he stands up and greets me. "Hey baby, so you call me out for a special dinner, how are you and how are things? I hope this is more than just a causal thing because I explain to you that a game isn't something I'm interested in. I need you to be all mines or not. What's going on babe?

"Jeff I am your woman. I am ready to leave Jimmy. My heart has already left him. I don't know how to go about it. I am ready to walk out the door. I don't have to go back if you don't want me to. I'll come with you right now." I don't trust him, and I don't want this kind of love anymore. I want to be loved as I love and be care for as I care. I love you babe and I am ready for the life and love you have to offer. I am serious Jeff I'm ready to be married to a good man a real man that really understands what love is.

Jeff looks at me and doesn't say anything and I wonder have I just made a fool of myself pouring out my heart and soul and maybe he was just bullshitting me all along. Tears start to fall and I can't seem to stop them this is enough I go from being a naive fool to a premeditated fool what the fuck. I stand up and I look at him. "I'm sorry that I've wasted your time and mine I thought you were serious about us and I guess I was mistaken. I will not contact you again" I walk away and he still sitting in the same spot and has not moved once. He is going to let me walk out the fucking door unbelievable. I am out done. I can't believe I was actually anticipating a life with this man and he was just a joke wow.

Chapter 13

WAT-EVER

I walking down the sidewalk and I'm crying my eyes out because I feel so stupid on both sides of the equation this can't be happening to me again. Then I hear Jeff calling my name. I don't want to talk now, are you serious what can he possible say. I walk a little faster can't run in these heels or I'd lose his ass. Brook stop for a minute babe, I was just shocked and I am ready to be the husband you deserve.

You don't know how many nights and days I've imagined you telling me you were ready for a real marriage a real commitment. I love you so much woman and I will show you that I love you and appreciate you." He pulls me close and I know he is serious. We kiss a long passionate kiss. Then I hear someone calling my name, I'm so caught up the voice sounded distant then it hit me, Jimmy was calling my name and he was snapping. What the fuck are you doing? Jeff are you kidding me, you trying to fuck my wife, in school you was a chump, now you want to be a player back up. Brook you gonna do me like that with this joke of a man, bitch I will beat your ass right here right now in front of this joke ass motherfucker you are my wife.

Jimmy I'm not your wife anymore, I'm his wife, fuck you, you clown ass nigga, you didn't think of me as your wife fucking them bitches making babies and got your freak as friend trying to fuck me. You didn't treat me like your wife when I wanted to be. Now I don't want to be your wife fuck you. Jimmy swings to hit me and Jeff blocks it and comes up with a right hook and Jimmy is on the ground. They are fighting Jimmy gets up quick and they are getting in,

I can't believe what I am seeing Kevin thought out loud, I thought this woman was a saint, here she is sneaking out on me and Jim with this dude, who the hell is this dude, Here I am following Jimmy collecting dirt on him when I should have been following her nut ass. She is sitting in the restaurant with this man. He seems to be ignoring her babble; something told me to follow this bitch tonight. I'm sitting across the street watching her. I should call Jim and tell him his nasty ass wife is just as nasty as he is. Out to fuck another dude and she didn't even give me a chance to prove to her that I'm the best for her, she off with another nigga, hell who is he? He isn't even one of us. I can't believe what I'm seeing my heart is crushed. I'm calling Jim right now. "Yo Jimmy boy I see your wife took a lesson out of your book she got herself a new man, now she down here eating dinner with the next man." Jimmy hangs up on me, but I know my boy he'll be down here in a few mins. This shit is on and popping now. Now she leaving, what, she is walking by herself, she looks upset. Maybe this dude is a lawyer or something, she probably filing for a divorce so she and I can be together. Ok now this dude is following her, I'm going to follow behind him to see what this is all about, what she kissing this man, unfucking believable. There is jimmy he about to fight this dude, all yawl all got it fuck up this is my bitch.

I can't believe Brook walked out and left me with the kids, I really can't get to mad though she is always with them and she is a good mother and wife, I guess she tired of my shit and now she hanging out with some new friends she met, These chicks come over all the time now. They are always handing out in the basement and playing cards. I really don't like it, but I guess I drove her to this new person she has become. All the children are asleep except Brooklyn and we are watching this cartoon she likes, the phone is ringing who this could be. "Hello, Kevin I know you not calling my house are you crazy man you a dead ass, what you mean she with another man. You are sick motherfucker and you better not be near my wife, I'll see you in a few mins." I can't leave little Brooklyn here alone and awake fuck it I'm take her with me. Brook you want to go for a ride with daddy we got to pick up your mom"

Araina D. Thompson

I know that is not my wife kissing another man, my eyes are playing tricks on me. I tell my daughter to stay in the car and as I get closer it is my wife with this nerd nigga Jeff.

Someone is grabbing my hair, swings me around and yells, look at yah two fagots fighting what's already mine. I'll kill both of you motherfuckers right now. Jeff pulls his gun, Jimmy pulls his gun and Kevin has his already out and I'm reaching for mine shots fired and everything going black and I feel myself falling as I look over I see my baby girl Brooklyn in the car screaming I couldn't hear her but I know she was screaming mommy. Its black I can't see anything I can't see my baby girl anymore.

ABOUT THE AUTHOR

My Name is Araina D. Thompson. I am a mother first
and foremost of five beautiful children. They are my
inspiration and my world. I became a parent at the
age of seventeen. My children and I kind of grew up together
in a sense that I was still a child myself. I was a responsible
child, and I took care of my children with the tools I had
and they took excellent care of me. They taught me what
family and loyally is all about and the value of unconditional love.
They gave me strength where there was none, and
they gave me a reason to move forward when I had
none. I owe my life and my success to my five children;
they made me see the world in a different light.

To my audience, nothing can stop your success, but you
know that you are your greatest asset.

Printed in the United States
By Bookmasters